an infinite love

"This is one of those books that is going to find you at the exact moment you need it. It brings you back to what your soul knows: self-love. Lisa is such a bright light for writing her personal experiences in a way that relates to all of us. At times I felt like my heart was opening just by reading her words."

—**HELEN MANN**,
blogger, @helenthegr8

"Lisa's enthusiastic grasp on life is infectious! In *An Infinite Love*, she never stops challenging us to rethink our beliefs and behaviors with love and compassion."

—**KATHY FISHER**,
certified professional coach

"If you're looking for easily digestible guidance for self-love, Lisa delivers. Lisa tells her story in such a unique way while weaving in life lessons and practical guidance for self-love. This book is a beautiful roadmap for anyone looking to navigate through life with more self-love."

—**KEVIN CRENSHAW**,
self-love coach, @the.heart.guy

Enjoy the book!

♡ Lisa Beck

YOUR JOURNEY TOWARD
HAMPINESS, CONNECTION, *and*
LOVING YOURSELF *the* MOST

---

an infinite love

LISA BECK

WISE INK

AN INFINITE LOVE © copyright 2020 by Lisa Beck. All rights reserved. No part of this book may be reproduced in any form whatsoever, by photography or xerography or by any other means, by broadcast or transmission, by translation into any kind of language, nor by recording electronically or otherwise, without permission in writing from the author, except by a reviewer, who may quote brief passages in critical articles or reviews.

ISBN 13: 978-1-63489-332-9
Library of Congress Catalog Number: 2020905741

Printed in the United States of America
First Printing: 2020

24 23 22 21 20   5 4 3 2 1

Cover design by Jessie Sayward Bright
Interior design by Kim Morehead

Wise Ink Creative Publishing
807 Broadway St NE
Suite 46
Minneapolis, MN, 55413

To order, visit www.itascabooks.com or call 1-800-901-3480.

Reseller discounts available.

SELF-LOVE:
Love for oneself that is more than just friends
—Urban Dictionary

This book is dedicated to my guardian angel, Grandma Sarvela; my first librarian, Auntie Fran; and fellow author Auntie Char. Grateful for your love and guidance in this world and beyond. Honored to have such amazing female role models.

Contents

Introduction	1
1. Time to Love Yourself More	7
2. Get Divorced . . . from Negativity	21
3. Toddlers . . . They're Doing Life Right	36
4. The Pursuit of Happiness Is an Inside Job	47
5. Find Your Mantra	57
6. Body Love	64
7. Building or Unbuilding a Routine	73
8. Find Your Passion	82
9. Love the Grass in Your Own Backyard	94
10. Lost and Not Found: Balance	101
11. Oh My God She's Naked	115
12. Be Your Own Hero	130
13. Be a Journey (Wo)Man	149
14. Cultivate Connection	158
Conclusion	168
Acknowledgments	171
About the Author	173

Introduction

I didn't know it at the time, but my journey to infinite love started in 2014. I was on a girls' trip to Philly, helping a friend with a charity event. I had never really been interested in getting a tattoo but for some reason felt like now, at thirty-three years old, was the time. I wasn't celebrating anything special. I didn't want to commemorate or memorialize anything. I just wanted to get one. Looking back, I now realize it was the Universe's way of starting me on my internal exploration of self-love.

I brought the tattoo idea up to the other girls, and the three of us decided we were all in. We booked our appointment and went on our way researching what our tattoos would be. Suddenly, I knew exactly what I wanted. I wanted an infinity symbol with the word *love* inscribed within.

One quick Pinterest search and you will see this is a common tattoo, so I wasn't winning any creative points. But it's what it represented that made it so special to me. I wanted a constant reminder that I am love, to love myself more, and to spread that love to others. Love is the one thing we can all use more of in our lives. Love drowns hate, brings light to darkness, and helps us find our way. We can lean on it during tough times. It perseveres above all else. I didn't know I needed a reminder to love myself more, but as I continued along this journey, I realized I truly did!

Seeing as I'm not much of a PDA person, I also thought my tattoo would be my form of nonverbal communication. By rubbing my hand over my tattoo, I'd be saying "I love you," either to myself or someone else, in my own language.

A BOOK IS BORN

It wasn't until three years after I got inked that I realized how life-changing and appropriate my little infinity sign with the word love inscribed was. That's when the real journey began. The journey of rediscovering myself, finding my way back to loving myself more, and experiencing a deep knowing of what true self-happiness means.

The idea of this book came to me one warm summer day as I was going for a walk. Walking is often my daily meditation. The creative juices flow, and I come up with many of my greatest ideas. The Universe—spirit, god, source, divine, intuition, call it what you will—connects with me the most during this time. I'm plugged in. But I didn't realize this until I started reading and learning more about spirituality and meditation, and meeting with healers and like-minded people. I was exploring and growing in my spiritual practice, and the more I grew, the more I accepted my special gifts, the more the Universe spoke to me.

I remember I was walking around my neighborhood when this idea popped into my head. *I should write a book on self-love.* A humorous, easy-to-read, real-life kind of book. Of course, I questioned this thought and said out

an infinite love

loud, "What a crazy idea! What do I know about self-love? What do I know about writing a book?" Then I started to realize that *of course* I'm supposed to write this book.

Working in the health and wellness industry, I help people goal set, overcome pain and obstacles, and watch them transcend physically, mentally, and emotionally. I've supported clients as they stood in front of me breaking down in pain and defeat, and I've jumped with jubilation as they experienced the high of accomplishment, self-satisfaction, and love. Many times, these highs and lows have nothing to do with exercise but, rather, with life events.

When you spend intimate time with someone and help to improve their life one plank at a time, walls come down and you experience every success and every failure together. I help them to realize that, often, to overcome physical pain or injury we have to look internally at the emotional tie. The issue in our tissue may be due to past events or trauma. Our bodies have a sneaky way of suppressing emotions and turning it into physical pain or injury.

I can physically aid in the healing of ligaments, tendons, and nerves—but the healing of emotional pain has to come from within. If I wanted to be of service to the best of my abilities to others, I had to go through the process and heal all of my emotional injuries. I had to recognize what it meant and felt like to heal. At the time, I wasn't quite sure what I was healing from. But, like in the pages of a great book, the plot twists were endless.

It became clear to me that, in order to heal yourself, you must have a deep, infinite love for yourself. Yet most people don't have a self-love practice and wouldn't recognize one or why they'd need it. The idea of loving yourself in order to heal yourself and thus letting the world experience your true greatness was not a common practice, and I wanted to make it so.

The voice in my head telling me to write this book was loud and kept calling to me. All of a sudden, I got really excited. As I thought about the process of writing a book, I realized that deep down I have always been a writer and it was time to rediscover my gift. After all, I was that kid growing up who wrote a ten-page story when everyone else only wrote two pages. I also started to realize I really *wanted* to write it. Midwalk, I stopped and sat down on a park bench to gather all my thoughts and capture the surge of energy flowing through me at the idea of creating a manuscript. Before I could make sense of it all, chapter titles came flooding into my brain. Before I even had a concept of an outline, I already had twenty chapter titles. For some of these chapter titles, I had enough words to fill a whole page at that instant. For others, I had no idea what they meant but knew I had to write them down. All I know is on that day I went walking, there was such a pull to write this book. I've never felt anything like it.

Later, as I sat down and attempted to figure out what each chapter title meant and how to navigate the journey, I realized this book was far more of a learning and living experience for me than I ever expected. Throughout the writing process, I discovered the pull and drive to get my thoughts on paper and navigate a story wasn't always strong. Quite often, I sat down to write and found I had nothing to say. I started to learn and recognize that part of my writer's block was based in ego and fear. Putting your thoughts and words on paper, knowing others may

an infinite love

read them one day, makes you really vulnerable. Digging deep to find the true meaning, asking yourself what lesson should be learned and how you can overcome, is hard. Especially when writing a book about self-love and realizing, *Wow, I needed some internal work in this area!* Memories, thoughts, and feelings came up, many of which had been suppressed for a long time and which I wasn't sure I wanted to revisit. Lots of eye-opening aha moments and *Wow, what's the root of that emotion?* Lots of *Go me!* and lots and lots of introspection.

We all have our strengths and weaknesses. Assessing them and recognizing them isn't always fun and can be a humbling experience. I've learned that self-forgiveness can be one of our biggest strengths and is essential in our healing. I've learned true happiness starts with self. I've learned that we hold the power inside of us to live the life we've always dreamed of. I've learned that we waste a lot—and I mean a *lot*—of energy on things, ideas, outcomes, and people who don't deserve an ounce of it. Imagine what we could do if we learned to redirect that energy into something more positive and deserving. I've learned that we're not made to go this journey alone, and community is vital to a higher quality of life. I believe our true journey is to learn and grow in all we do, and that is exactly what this book has been for me: a way to learn and grow beyond self.

To love unconditionally means to love someone no matter what. We love our children, pets, family, and even friends unconditionally, but do we love ourselves this way? Without condition, from the deep, dark, scary crevices to the bliss-filled moments, with every heartbreak and accomplishment and everywhere in between? We must love ourselves through it all. It is my wish that, through these pages, you take the journey with me in rediscovering an infinite love for yourself.

THE LOWDOWN

Here's how to use this book: Each chapter is filled with personal stories and lessons I've learned along the way that helped me to overcome my fears and self-doubt, and allowed me to love and accept myself to the fullest. At the end of each chapter are ways you can take action to help emphasize the lessons learned. As with many self-development books, some ideas are repeated throughout. Sometimes it takes seeing or hearing a lesson multiple times or in a different context for it to really sink in. There are many actions that involve journaling, so it would be helpful to have a notebook or journal handy while reading this book. I understand that not everyone learns the same way, so I tried to incorporate other actionable modalities you can use if writing isn't your medium. It is my goal that this book becomes a constant learning tool that you can refer to again and again. You may choose to read the book cover to cover, following all the lessons and calls to action, or you may start by randomly flipping to a page. There are no rules. Trust that whatever chapter and lesson you land on, that is what you are meant to learn. Old patterns don't change overnight, so be patient with yourself as you tackle the lessons that speak to you. Know that just by picking up this book, you are saying yes to yourself. Yes to loving yourself more and yes to an abundant life. Share your experience and lessons learned with others. You never know the impact you can have on someone. Let the journey begin.

CHAPTER ONE

Time to Love Yourself More

"Your task is not to seek for love but merely to seek and find all of the barriers within yourself which you have built against it."
—Helen Schucman

A couple years ago, I was having coffee with a friend, and she asked me if I was dating anyone. At that point, dating someone was the last thing on my mind. I was in a funk—not with dating but with myself. Something was missing, and I couldn't put a finger on it. Outwardly, no one saw anything different; I looked the same and went about my daily routine as normal. But on the inside, I was kind of a mess. I was lost and searching.

I began to realize I just wasn't *in love* with who I was, and if I didn't even love myself, how could I expect someone else to love me? I wasn't sure what I didn't love about myself, but I felt off, a little burnt out on life, and not filled with internal happiness.

lisa beck

My mind started firing questions. *How did this happen? When did it start? What does truly being in love with yourself even look like? What qualities, characteristics, and fears do I have that are hindering my personal growth and total love of self? What old stories am I telling myself? How do I show up for myself, and how do I fix this issue that I can't even put my finger on?*

I recognized that I needed to get back to falling in love with me. Then and only then would I truly be a good partner and attract the right people and right opportunities in my life.

THE DISEASE TO PLEASE

I got back to loving myself by starting to write this book. I was researching self-love, reading other authors, listening to podcasts and life coaches and relationship experts, and having discussions with friends. In an aha moment, I discovered I had a classic case of the "disease to please," as Oprah calls it. I was turning to everyone and everything else in search of validation and self-love when I needed to search internally. I was giving, giving, giving—my time, my energy, and my resources—to others without filling my heart in return.

I found that, at times, I was too caught up in the stories I was telling myself and out of tune with reality. I wanted to learn how to be truly happy for others and their successes and stop comparing my journey to theirs. I wanted to learn to be vulnerable and open up my heart to others, to stand in my own power and take the risk, and to be and believe in my true authentic self. I wanted to learn to love myself first and to turn back to love—back to loving myself.

Lesson one: Loving yourself more starts internally.

an infinite love

BEGIN TO DATE YOURSELF

As I turned back to love, I decided I needed to start at the beginning—and the beginning of every great relationship starts with a date. I needed to date myself. One night, I met some girlfriends for dinner and they all commented, "Lis, you're dressed to impress! Why so fancy?" They were correct: I was dressed to impress. But I wasn't trying to impress them, a man, or anyone else, for that matter. The only person I wanted to impress was myself.

Work in the health and wellness industry can be very masculine. As much as I thoroughly enjoy the ease and comfort of my everyday clothes, there isn't much femininity in yoga pants, a zip-up, and a baseball cap. I knew I needed to embrace my feminine side more, so I made a point to do so at any chance I had. I also made sure to make time for me, do things that made me happy, get to know myself again, be patient with myself, and forgive, acknowledge, and embrace my idiosyncrasies. Just as if I were dating a man.

During my self-dating process, another one of my aha moments came after my sister sent me a text: "Hey, check out this poet I started following on Instagram @atticuspoetry. I just ordered his book. He writes some really good stuff!" So of course, I looked him up and two short epigrams caught my eye, as they spoke to exactly what I needed to do and did. He writes: "Never go in search of love, go in search of life, and life will find you the love you seek."

Too often, we settle, not only in romantic relationships but also in life. Think of the people you know who have settled for a job, settled for a partnership, settled for a particular town or city they may not enjoy, settled for the wrong meal at a restaurant, or settled for whatever misfortunes life has thrown their way. They are playing small, and life is meant to be played big—real big! I believe most of these settlements are based out of fear, not knowing the outcome, and the what-ifs. How miserable we would be if we based our entire life on the what-ifs. We wouldn't do anything. These choices are not based out of love for ourselves. We deserve more!

Search for life, dare to dream, and take steps to make that dream a reality. When you search for life, love will follow—a love of what you do, where you live, and life in general. A search for life is also a deep search for who you are at a soul level.

Lesson two: When you fall in love with yourself, you fall in love with life.

GIRL, DON'T GO LOSING YOURSELF

The other short poem @atticuspoetry wrote that really caught my eye was this: "Don't find her and lose you, find you to find her." I believe this can relate to many different situations. Initially reading this poem, I think of a man searching. Searching for a woman and wishing, hoping, praying so hard for his true partner that he completely forgets who he is and what he stands for and again settles for what comes along. We all know people who are in relationships like this. One of the partners has completely lost themselves and fallen out of love with themselves along the way. They are looking to another to find themselves.

I also believe this short poem can speak to new parents—new mothers especially. How many new mothers do you know that have lost themselves in the care of their

an infinite love

children? They have a baby, and poof . . . it's like they disappeared off the face of the earth! Unless you have children the same age and can provide a playdate, good luck seeing them for the next eighteen years. I get it. Life changes, roles change, and your life has a whole new meaning now. Just don't lose *you* in the process. Find you to find her.

What are your needs? Do you need social activities, adult conversations, and continued support from others to help you in being a better parent? I don't believe anyone who says they don't. How can you bring your best self and love without end to your children if you don't love yourself first? Every part of you, the good, the bad, and the ugly.

Lesson three: Love is the essence of our lives, but it starts with ourselves.

STOP, HOLD UP, YOU'RE PROJECTING

When author, researcher, and speaker Brené Brown tells audiences that parents should not love their children more than they love themselves, she finds that parents get pretty hostile. She says these reactions tend to come from parents of innocent young kids rather than parents of teens, as parents of teens start to see characteristics in their children that bother them in themselves or their partner. I agree 100 percent with Brown and believe, like her, that parents' reactions are based on both love and fear: love of their child and desire to provide the best life for them, and fear that they can't.

Every parent wants their children to grow up strong, smart, confident, and fully aware of their self-worth.

lisa beck

When I was young, I was a voracious reader. Our library had a summer reading program, and there were prizes based on how many pages you read. I would go to the library and get *stacks*—I mean stacks—of books. I wanted to win the top prize (which, mind you, was probably a pencil and an eraser, but damn it, I wanted to be the top reader in my small town). I would sit on my couch all day reading as my sister was running around the yard with the neighborhood gang. My mom would put a time limit on my reading and make me go outside and play. I would get so upset about this. I was a good kid and wasn't doing anything wrong. But alas, telling her that never seemed to work. She wanted me to get exercise, which, in hindsight, I completely understand. Oddly enough, exercise ended up being the career field I gravitated toward.

I also understand that part of her reaction was based on the fact that she didn't have many friends when she was young and didn't want me to have to go through that. What she couldn't understand, or didn't see, was that I felt I had plenty of friends whom I could dial up anytime I wanted and was quite content for the current moment enjoying my books. I was on a top-reader-of-the-town mission, for goodness' sake. Her struggles as a youth weren't mine. Even though she and my dad did an amazing job raising two strong, smart, confident young girls surrounded by love, she lost sight of that and was projecting her fears onto me.

I can see how unconditional love causes you to move mountains to show love for and protect your children. It takes a lot of personal self-work to take a step back, love from afar, and recognize when you are projecting your

an infinite love

hurt, fear, and struggles onto your children or others and not embracing their unique characteristics. Love yourself first, and your children will follow suit.

Lesson four: When you are out of love with yourself, you may project your fears onto other areas of your life.

BEING IMPERFECT IS QUITE PERFECT

When my sister's boyfriend decided to propose to her, his mother warned him, "You know those sisters are very close. You aren't just marrying one of them. You're marrying both!" I like to tease him that it was the best two-for-one deal he would ever come across, but I have to say I hit the jackpot in the brother-in-law lottery. He has been such a great addition to our family.

Lura, my sister, called me the other day as she was driving home from work. We were both stressed and complaining to each other. The holidays were fast approaching, and we both felt we had so much on our plates that we weren't sure how we'd get everything done in time. In the midst of our discussion, Lura mentioned a recent conversation she had with her husband. "Joe says we set our expectations too high." At first, I thought, *What the heck is he talking about? Of course we set the bar high. I expect big things for myself, fully believing in my capabilities. So yes, my expectations are high.*

She then went on to explain, "He said we, you and I, often place these expectations on ourselves—whether to appease ourselves, family, friends, society, or whoever—and sometimes they are just unreachable or unrealistic. We stress ourselves out attempting to reach them, and if we don't reach them, then we feel like a failure. But in whose eyes?"

I was about to argue, but then it hit me like a tree branch to the face. He was 100-percent right. My sister and I project our fear of failure and being judged as not good enough by creating very high expectations for ourselves. We're worried about the reactions of others if we don't measure up. After recognizing this, it sounded absurd. Are our parents going to love us any less if we don't use the good china for a holiday meal? Are our friends going to stop calling if we say, "No, I can't meet for dinner because I have too much on my plate right now"? Is our family going to stop supporting us if we quit the jobs we hate? A big, fat, hairy *no*! And, if they did, that would say way more about them than it did about us.

Having high expectations can be a great thing, as it means we want more from and for ourselves. We recognize our own worth. But when expectations are set based on the acceptance and love from others, that's when we can get into trouble.

On the inside cover of my journal, I wrote, "Love yourself for all you do, for who you are, who you will become and for all your faults because they make you you and that is what the world wants to see," so that I see, feel, and read it every day. It helps me to see being imperfect is absolutely perfect!

Lesson five: Loving yourself more is recognizing and managing the origins of your expectations.

DRINKING THE JUNGLE JUICE
Things were starting to get serious in this relationship with

an infinite love

myself, and I knew that in order to keep moving forward and get back to loving myself more, I needed to take an action of love. I'm the type of person who enjoys change, a challenge, learning, traveling, and growing personally and professionally. When that isn't happening, I'm not my best self.

One day, a friend sent me an Instagram message. "Hey, check out this yoga retreat in Costa Rica! Doesn't that sound fun?" The theme of the retreat was "Purpose and Passion." This was exactly what I was searching for: my purpose, my direction, and how to get there. I had to go. Fear crept up, saying, *What the heck are you doing? This trip is expensive. Do you have the money? Do you have the time? You'd be traveling by yourself.* Blah blah blah. But something in me said I had to do this. After all, it checked all the boxes: challenge, learning, travel, and personal growth. I needed to do this for myself, to take action for me, to get back to loving myself. So I took the leap and signed myself up, thinking, *Costa Rica, here I come!*

Lindsay, our fearless Unicorn Leader, radiated love, light, energy, and passion from the inside out. When you are ready, the right people come into your life at exactly the right moment, and she was the perfect person to lead the way. A former executive coach in Canada, she left the corporate scene to make an impact on the world by speaking, teaching, and leading others to find their passion and purpose. Part of this was bringing ten strangers together in the jungles of Costa Rica. Throughout the retreat, she had us write little sticky notes of encouragement and affirmations to all participants. As we were leaving on the last day, we each received an envelope filled with sticky notes—little love notes from our new friends for us to read on our travels home.

These little notes caught me by surprise because each one said similar things about me. Strong, wise, and powerful, with a soft, graceful beauty, like a female warrior. Why didn't I see these traits in myself even though ten strangers saw them in me in a short period of time? I didn't realize it, but I was internalizing my fears that I was not good enough, couldn't measure up, and wasn't loveable. I had a choice: I could continue living in my fear or wake up and realize all these positive characteristics and more were true. I am a powerful being, and I needed to step into that power. I am that, that is me!

The funny thing is that I would never have considered myself an insecure person. I felt that I so strongly believed in myself and who I was, yet with this exercise I saw that there was some doubt in me, some icky messes to clean up, and some healing to be done. I decided then and there I wanted to believe so wholeheartedly in myself that I was bursting at the seams and there was no turning back. To this day, I keep these sticky notes in an envelope in my journal and pull them out when I need to be reminded of my female warrior status. Wonder Woman, you looking for a partner?

Lesson six: Learn to love yourself more by believing and seeing yourself the way your loved ones do.

SPEAK YOUR OWN LOVE LANGUAGE

On my journey to love myself more, I had to ask myself how I showed and received love. I recognized that not everyone spoke the same love language and that under-

an infinite love

standing how my loved ones showed love and affection would help me to receive their love with a better understanding and a fuller heart. *If honoring someone else's love language helped me to love them more*, I wondered, *wouldn't that also work on myself?* If I showed myself love through my personal love language, wouldn't that strengthen my relationship with myself? So I began to do just that.

Dr. Gary Chapman's bestseller *The 5 Love Languages* talks about five universal ways people express and interpret love. People tend to give love the way they prefer to receive love. Recognizing these five love languages — words of affirmation, acts of service, quality time, physical touch, and receiving gifts — will help you to communicate your wants and needs more effectively, not only to others but also to yourself.

One of my love languages is physical touch. If you're like me, you can honor this by treating yourself to massage and facials. Hug and snuggle those you love. Buy a soft, fuzzy blanket or robe and wrap yourself in it each night. Surround yourself with items that feel good to touch.

If you speak love via receiving gifts, give yourself something special. It doesn't have to be big, just a small item showing yourself love and appreciation. I have a friend who buys herself fresh flowers every week. A small act of giving to herself!

For acts of service, hire someone to take a task off of your to-do list. Better yet, find a friend who speaks this love language and ask for help. Trust me, as someone who speaks this language, helping someone out in a time of need can bring joy to both parties. Never be afraid to ask for help. Don't be a martyr. No one can do it all. There

lisa beck

will always be someone around willing to give a helping hand. You just need to ask.

For words of affirmation, journal or write yourself a love note. Buy some positive affirmation cards and make a pact to start your day reading one. Listen to positive affirmation meditations or podcasts. Create a positive quote board. I mentioned previously in this chapter the sticky notes of self-love; you can write these yourself and place positive affirmations all around your house.

Quality time is an easy one in regard to showing yourself love. Spend time alone, doing what you love to do. Ignore your to-do list, put the chores aside for a while, and just enjoy being with yourself. My friend Carrie is an early riser, and the morning is her time to be by herself. Before her family wakes, she may catch up on her shows, do something creative, read, or go for a walk. By the time her family wakes, she is refreshed and ready to take on the day.

We all speak love in different ways. Recognize these ways in others and in yourself. Doing so will strengthen your connection and love for yourself. Isn't that what we all want—love and connection?

In order to give deep love, you better be willing to receive love in return. So many people have a hard time accepting love into their life. I'm talking about deep, soul-connecting love not only with others but also with yourself. Not everyone is willing to hand out that kind of love, but I think fewer people are actually willing to receive it. They think they are but, deep down, don't actually believe they are worthy of this type of love. In order to receive that kind of love—an earth-shattering, mind-quak-

an infinite love

ing, body-shaking kind of love—you better be willing to give that kind of love to yourself. Only then, by believing you are worthy of a to-the-ends-of-the-earth type of love, will you be able to attract that into your life. Believing is seeing and receiving. To love yourself is to love others. You are worth it. Believe it, and then receive it!

Lesson seven: Learning and speaking your own love language can create deeper connections with yourself and other loved ones.

CONCLUSION

Love is kind, love is heart, love is vulnerability, love is humorous, love is light, love is trust, love is honesty, love is laughter, love is forgiveness, love is spirituality, love is fun, love is pain, love is pleasure, love is cloudy, love is clear, love comes from within, love is meant to be shared. Love is meant to be shouted, love is meant to be whispered. Love is unexpected, love is obvious. Love is energy. Love is high vibrations. Walk in love and feel it surround you. Drown yourself in its magic. Love is all around us; we just have to open our eyes, be aware of our surroundings, and trust in the journey and in the process.

As the wonderful and wise Dr. Seuss wrote, "Today you are you, that is truer than true. There is no one alive who is youer than you." I'm going to add, "If you don't love you, then who?"

CALL TO ACTION

Take inventory of your life. Journal answers to these questions:
- Where are you not giving yourself the highest levels of love and appreciation?
- Are you letting certain people off the hook in how they show you love? Who and why?
- Are you letting yourself off the hook?
- Are you setting expectations looking for approval from someone else? Who and why?
- In which areas of your life are you settling? Why?

Journal about a time you felt you lost a part of yourself.
- What could you have done to feel more seen or heard?

Journal about areas of your own life in which you may be projecting your fears.

Take the love language quiz and make a regular practice of honoring yourself via your love language: www.5lovelanguages.com/quizzes.

CHAPTER TWO

Get Divorced . . . from Negativity

"You have been criticizing yourself for years, and it hasn't worked. Try approving of yourself and see what happens."

—Louise Hay

"What? You're writing a book on self-love and you just uttered those dreadful words, 'Get divorced'?"

You better believe I did! If it—i.e., your career, organization, friend, mindset, habit, fear, or relationship—isn't serving you to be your best, highest self, take the Big D! Divorce him, her, it, the feelings, the situation, or the negativity. Life is energy, people are energy, and things are energy, and once you start raising your vibration, anything that's not vibing at your frequency must go.

HAPPY HOLIDAYS, LOVE THE FORGETMENOTS

Once, a numerologist / business coach mentioned that I would get divorced a few times in my life. I was freaked out, as I hadn't even been married yet someone was already dooming my future relationships. Who wants to go into a relationship knowing they will eventually be getting divorced? Not I! I was already struggling with commitment at that point, and those words surely did not help. But one day, I realized that a few of my relationships with friends and acquaintances were changing, and there were some people I just didn't want to hang out with anymore. They didn't do anything to me, nor me to them; we were moving in different directions, and our time was up. You know, that whole "some people come into our lives for a reason, a season, a lifetime" quote. I didn't truly resonate with that quote until I experienced it for myself. Friends who once were practically a part of me are now a card at Christmas and a text exchange here and there. At first, I was sad and hurt. To have someone so near and dear "divorce" me and to realize our relationship was changing really stung. It took me a while to realize my own fears of disconnection, unlovability, and worthiness were tied up in these divorces.

After recognizing this, I was able to accept that just because our relationships now look different doesn't mean they are any less special to me or I to them. Today I am really happy with our relationships and realize how important their roles are in my life. I cherish our memories and past together.

In every person, career, or situation we find ourselves, we can also find a lesson to learn and grow. An opportunity to level up. Search for that inner guiding voice, and listen to what it is saying. If that voice says you've outgrown this, that you are not happy, or that it does not serve you anymore, it is time to move forward. We must listen! It is

an infinite love

crucial we get clear with who or what is not serving us and what our intuition is telling us to leave behind. This inner voice has our best interest at heart and knows the path for us. Intuitively, we know when something just isn't working anymore. What's difficult is taking the steps to love yourself enough to recognize this and move on. Like I recognized that my own fears were tied up in my "divorce," it's important for each of us to take the time to recognize why something isn't serving us anymore. Figure out what attachments need to change and how to move forward with kindness, love of self, and forgiveness.

Lesson one: Listen to your intuition and recognize when it's time to make a change.

I CAN'T SEE. IT'S TOO DARK!

Sometimes part of that change involves what I call "taking a walk in the darkness." Take a moment and recognize how you feel. Deep down, what frightens you? Don't be afraid. Embrace the dark. Learn in the dark. Explore the dark. The light will shine on. Find the light, be the light, and call the light toward you. The light will always come, but you have to do work to find it. Search deep within your soul, and you will find it.

I used to be afraid of being alone. Like *alone* alone. Growing up, I had bad FOMO (fear of missing out). Let me clarify: I'm perfectly fine being by myself and sometimes rather enjoy it, but I'd rather be with someone. And I don't mean in a sexual manner—it could be a friend, a partner, or family. Someone to enjoy just being with. Someone with whom I can cocreate ideas, discussion, joy, and humor.

Because I live alone and work one-on-one with others, I spend most of my day alone. Sometimes I miss people. I'm also a pretty impulsive and spontaneous person. I get an idea and want to run with it. In my twenties, it was fun and I could always find a friend to go along with one of my crazy plans. Now in my midthirties, most of my friends have kids or other adult responsibilities, so being spontaneous takes a bit of planning.

As I took a walk in my own darkness and dug deep into my fear of being alone and missing out, I began to appreciate qualities about myself I seemed to have overlooked: my creativity, my spontaneity, my go-with-the-flow attitude, and my contentment. I found my fear lessening and JOMO—joy of missing out—starting to set in.

Another journey I took in my darkness was recognizing my fear around money. I had two major fears when it came to making money: I was afraid of assigning too high of a value to my services, and I was afraid that I didn't deserve all that I was worth. I didn't believe in what I was selling (me), and if I didn't believe in it, then of course no one else would. This is a self-worth hiccup that we will unpack more in a later chapter.

Growing up, we didn't have a lot of money. From a young age, I learned the importance of saving, spending within your limits, and differentiating a need from a want. All three can be very valuable lessons. However, my second fear of money can also be attributed to this. I had a lack mentality. A panic mentality that there wasn't and wouldn't be enough money to meet my needs. Lack doesn't attract, it repels. What you think, you believe; what you believe, you achieve. In order to attract anything into your

an infinite love

life—love, money, opportunities, what have you—you must have an abundant mindset. A mindset that emphasizes what you currently have is enough but recognizes there are unlimited possibilities available to you.

By recognizing and confronting these two fears—ending up alone and a lack of money—my whole perspective changed and I found I was content in where and who I was. Divorcing negativity and taking a walk through my darkness led to self-acceptance, happiness, increased income, and love. So much love that it became my mission to spread love to others.

Lesson two: Walking in the darkness brings old fears to light, allowing self-healing and acceptance to begin.

FORGIVENESS IS MY FAVORITE F-WORD

We've all been there, right? Dated, married, or partnered, whether literally or figuratively, with someone or something that didn't bring out the best in us. We got so immersed and wrapped up in pleasing, being accepted, filling a role, and meeting the needs of others that we became blind. Blind to the fact that we were shutting important people out. Those that were there for us through the good and the bad and those that already accepted and loved us for who we were became nonexistent or not a priority. It takes major courage and vulnerability to admit you were blind. To be humble and vulnerable enough to reach out and say you're sorry takes strength, but the absolute freedom that comes with opening yourself up and being willing to divorce the negative attachments makes it worth every tear and fear.

The funny thing is, those that really do care about you

appreciate the act of being vulnerable more than the words "I'm sorry." That, to me, shows you are making yourself a priority, learning, and growing from choices you made that don't sit right with you. Those that do care will forgive, and those that don't and need more . . . well, they're not meant to be in your life, and it's time for a divorce.

If someone shuts you out—whether it was your child, friend, significant other, or coworker—practice forgiveness. Show them love and kindness. Be their guide. Guide them back to the person they once were. Show them the reason you love and appreciate them. Help them love themselves. We are all human, after all. We all make mistakes and forget who we are and what we deserve in life.

If you are the person who got lost along the way, my advice to you is to take a look inside yourself. Ask the hard questions. Walk in the darkness. Find and surround yourself with people who will raise you up, tell you the truth, and support you through it. Most importantly, forgive yourself. Treat yourself with love, compassion, and devotion. There is freedom in letting go, forgiving yourself, and moving forward. We shouldn't carry our burdens into our future.

Lesson three: Practicing forgiveness of self and others will lead to more internal happiness.

BOUNDARIES AREN'T JUST FOR SOCCER FIELDS

As I divorced one job and started another, I had a lot more freedom in my schedule and decided I wanted to spend some of my time volunteering. I did my research and found a wonderful local nonprofit that was a perfect fit. Pretty soon, I was volunteering on a regular basis, and

an infinite love

that led to becoming an employee and then chairing fundraising events. I have a hard time saying no, and because I cared so much for this organization, I was willing to give, give, give—to my own detriment. I noticed that I started feeling resentment and didn't enjoy my time with the organization anymore. I didn't set up healthy boundaries for myself, and that led to my complete burnout.

Even if we have the best intentions and want to help the worthiest causes, it's imperative we set up boundaries for self-preservation. Setting up boundaries for ourselves, with others, and around situations can prevent the negativity from seeping in.

Although I talk a lot about divorce throughout this chapter—divorce this, divorce that—I also understand that sometimes we just aren't able to divorce certain people or things. It is in these situations that it becomes even more imperative to create boundaries for yourself. In what areas of your life do you have healthy boundaries set up, and in what areas of your life do you need to create more?

I'm an empath, and I enjoy helping people. But in the past, I had unhealthy boundaries around this. I found that, in relationships—any kind of relationship, but especially in the romantic realm—I would try to "save" people. Take their pain, hardship, or struggles away. Fix things for them. Help them to heal. Unfortunately, it looked a little bit like this: *Oh, you have baggage. So do I. Here, let me carry all the bags, including mine. I'll unpack them all for you, cook you dinner, and while I'm at it, how about dessert? Don't worry about unpacking my bags; maybe I'll find some time eventually to do that, but you first, always.* So unhealthy for everyone! After I recognized this, I realized healing is a choice everyone needs to make from within and I can't help them if they aren't ready for it. What I needed to say was, *Oh you have baggage? Me too! Let's carry our own luggage and slowly unpack it together. Maybe this way we can be smarter about our baggage and won't have so much to unpack in the future.*

Healthy boundaries can look different for everyone. You need to find what works for you. I'm continually working on setting and sticking to my boundaries. Start recognizing the signs when your boundaries are being crossed. For me, when I start to feel overwhelmed, anxiety-ridden, resentful, angry, desperate, or pressured, I take inventory. If these feelings are due to the lack of a boundary, it's time for me to take action for myself.

The biggest lesson I've learned is that it's OK to say no. No, I deserve to be treated better. No, now is not a good time for me to take on that role. No, I can't make it on the girls' weekend. No, I am unable to attend that event. No, no, no! Not now. Even if I really wanted to be a part of all mentioned items, they would all add to my already overcrowded plate and cause me stress and anxiety. I need to continually stand up for myself. I need to be my best self for everything I do, and in order to do that, I had to learn to say no. As a mentor of mine says, "If it's not a hell yes, it's a hell no!" I try to follow this mantra regularly.

Lesson four: Setting healthy boundaries sets you up for a healthy and happy life.

SLOW YOUR ROLL AND LOSE CONTROL

Getting divorced takes a lot of inside work, self-forgiveness, and courage. Along with people, I've also divorced habits

an infinite love

that weren't serving me (or we are currently separated, at least). I've divorced foods that were hurting my digestive system. I've divorced fitness studios that weren't aligned with my goals. I've divorced career choices that were no longer a good fit.

Maybe most importantly for me, I've divorced outcomes. I like control. I like to be in control. I like to know what is going to happen. I'm the person who immediately turns to the last page in a book and reads the ending. Part of that is my natural leadership mentality, but I also recognize the subconscious act of controlling the situation allows me to reach my expectations. However, sometimes life doesn't work out that way. When we try to hold onto control and manipulate the outcome, more often than not all we do is end up overwhelmed or disappointed.

To be honest, my life is nothing like I'd thought it would be at this age, and I've come to the realization that I don't know the outcome of my own story. I always assumed I'd follow the proverbial life ladder: college, grad school, job, a husband somewhere in there, then house and kids. When that didn't happen, I panicked.

I've had to learn to release control of the outcomes and go with the flow. I've learned to surrender to the faith that, if I work hard and live with an open heart, there is a plan for me and I'm exactly where I need to be. I've found this leads to way less stress and way more self-acceptance. Also, it turns out that proverbial life ladder wasn't for me anyway. I was feeling all the pressure to live someone else's timeline. I can say that, because I've learned to release control and manage my expectations, I'm currently living and creating a life I couldn't be more proud of or happier to be living. For me, releasing control started with writing in a journal, practicing gratitude, taking care of my mind and body, and speaking with my inner circle—people who I can always trust to give me loving and honest feedback. I also continue to practice focusing on the only things I can control: my thoughts, words, and actions. I try to live more in the present. Living in the past can be based on fear, and living in the future brings on anxiety, but living in the present is living in joy and flow.

Lesson five: Release control and go with the flow.

WORDS MATTER

The words you speak, the words you hear, the words you feel—they all matter! They impact others and they impact you, in both a positive and negative manner. Words matter. Speak like you believe it.

We all know little kids are like sponges. They pick up on everything. Even when we don't think they're listening, they are. They are watching us like hawks and pick up on even the smallest things. Let's not forget that and be conscious of how we speak to our partners, how we speak to ourselves, what our fears are, what we celebrate, how we carry ourselves, and what habits we form. They are always watching and always learning.

One day, my friend's daughter saw me drinking coffee. She looked shocked and right away said, "You can't drink that! Coffee's only for dads, and you're not a dad!" In her world, only her father drank coffee, and that meant only dads drink coffee. Another friend of mine drove past a golf course every day when she and her daughter were exiting their neighborhood. After weeks of driving past

an infinite love

this golf course, her daughter chimed in and, with utter shock, said, "Mommy, girls can play golf?" Her mom, royally confused, responded, "Of course, honey. Girls can do anything they want to. Why do you ask?" Her daughter noted that every day they'd driven past the golf course and she'd only ever seen men golf, but today she saw a woman! What our children see and don't see matters. What we are saying—and in these two cases, not saying—to our children matters.

Many times, children see arguments or fights between parents, family members, other adults—but what they don't often see is the making up. Most making up doesn't happen right away or happens behind closed doors, on the phone, or via email. Not in front of the children. If you think children don't pick up on the negative energy surrounding an argument, you are wrong. What type of impact do you think that has on their little growing brains and subconscious?

In my decision to be happier, be more self-aware, and love myself more, I've made a conscious effort to change my language and divorce the negative pessimistic talk. I've noticed that even a subtle change of words changes my whole perspective and elevates my mood. I imagine it's changing brain function as well. When something is hard, instead of saying I can't do it, I say it's a challenge for me. I acknowledge the activity, sentiment, task, or whatever it may be is hard, but I don't frame my sentences from a negative space. To me, "I can't" says "I give up, I suck," whereas "This is a challenge" says "This is hard but I'm willing to try. I may not be perfect, but I'm not stopping."

When having a disagreement with others, instead of

telling them they made me angry, upset, or frustrated, I say "I feel [angry, upset, frustrated] because of when you . . ."

The first example blames and attacks the other person. Most likely, the other person will react defensively or with contempt, shut down, or claim victimhood. All leading to the further breakdown of a relationship. The second example shows the other person how their actions make you feel. They have no control over how you feel and generally don't want you to feel negative emotions, so they are more willing to have a continued discussion. This way also shows respect and creates a safe space for continued dialogue. These are proven tactics in having crucial conversations.

We talk to ourselves, in our head or out loud, more than we talk to anyone else, and much of our self-talk is negative. *I'm not smart enough. I can't do it. I'm not strong enough. I'm not worthy of their love and affection. They don't get me. Don't stand out, I'll be judged. My thighs are too big. My boobs aren't big enough.* And so on and so on. Why do we do this? Why do we constantly speak negatively to ourselves? Do we say this type of thing to our friends and loved ones? No! We encourage and lift them up.

When you find yourself ambushed by that sneaky little devil, make a list of everything that you love and that brings joy to your life. From that list, take one thing and say it out loud. Your thoughts and words become the energy of your life. Positive thoughts and words create positive energy. Get out of your own way, and let the energy flow! Choose positivity and love.

Whenever you find a situation in which you are get-

an infinite love

ting down on yourself, just think of someone close to you and say out loud, "Would I say these words about them to their face?" I believe it's easier to catch your words when speaking to someone else than it is to control the words you speak to yourself. We need to learn to change the language. For example: "I am stupid" is different than "I feel stupid when . . ."

"I am stupid" insinuates stupidity in all actions at all times and will continue to release negative low vibrations, whereas "I feel stupid when" acknowledges one particular action. You are the only one in control of your words, thoughts, and actions. Self-sabotaging words, thoughts, and actions need to go. Give them the Big D! Remember, where your thoughts go, energy flows. Put time and energy into positive, uplifting, supportive, loving thoughts and actions, especially toward yourself.

Like we did during my Costa Rica yoga retreat, pick ten people who know you and ask them to write down three strength words or a short phrase that describes you on a sticky note. I want you to see what others see. It shouldn't be a shock to read these lovely words of affirmation about ourselves, yet for a lot of us it is. Let's change that!

Place these ten sticky notes of love wherever you need them the most—on the bathroom mirror so you see them every time you walk into the bathroom, on your laptop, in your underwear drawer, in a jacket pocket. When it's time to pull out my winter coats for the season, I never know what I'll find hiding in the pockets from the previous year. If I haven't had my coat dry cleaned, it's usually tissues, lip balm, and loose change. Every now and then, I'll find five, ten, or even twenty dollars. Any day you pull out random cash you didn't know you had is the best day ever. Why can't it be a little sticky note of love you pull out of your jacket pocket? A note you forgot you placed in there that, upon reading, lights up your day. It's never a bad time or wrong place to practice positive words of affirmation about yourself. That is loving yourself the most!

Someone is always listening to what you have to say. More often than not, it's the people you have the biggest influence on: family, friends, children, and yourself. Make a conscious effort to change the way you think and speak to honor and love yourself more. I've noticed that, with just this simple task, I am way more thoughtful with my words when speaking to myself and others. I am leading with my heart when I speak, and that is leading with love.

Lesson six: The words you speak matter. Divorce the negative talk. Speak from love and not from fear.

CALL TO ACTION

In your everyday language, practice speaking more from self-love.
- Write down an example of when you spoke from fear, hurt, or shame and how you could turn your words around so you spoke from love.

Reflect on areas of your life in which you try to control the outcome.
- Ask yourself what is behind this need for control.

Practice breathing techniques, journaling, yoga, conversations with friends, or meditations to help calm the nervous system and relinquish control.

Create healthy boundaries for yourself.

Make a commitment to remove self-sabotaging thoughts, words, and actions from your mindset.

Have ten people write out sticky notes of love to you—or do it yourself—and place them in random places.

Make social time for the people in your life who lift you up.
- Have open discussions with them about negative self-talk, how often you catch yourself doing it, and what you can do about it.

CHAPTER THREE

Toddlers ... They're Doing Life Right

"You make your life hard by always being in your head. Life is simple, get out of your head and get into the moment."

—Sylvester McNutt III

When we lose our authentic self, we forget to play. We become "busy" and self-conscious. When asked by others, "How's life?", isn't our response typically that we're busy? And sure, we are busy working, bringing kids here and there, taking care of responsibilities, etc. But are we really *that* busy, or are we just saying it because it signifies that we have it all together and can handle so much? I'll make a to-do list that is nearly impossible to accomplish and then say that I'm so busy. But am I really, or am I making myself seem busy to fill a need or void? I was self-conscious about not seeming busy, as if that meant I was lazy, unintelligent, or unproductive. In making myself

an infinite love

so busy, I was aiming to appease others and totally forgetting about myself along the way.

PLAYERS GONNA PLAY, PLAY, PLAY

Because we are so "busy," we often forget to play. Play was built into my leadership retreats in both Costa Rica and Kenora, Ontario. Specific time built in to remind us to be kids again. In Costa Rica, we surfed, rode bikes, danced, and even took a primal movement class where we got on the floor and rolled around like animals. While in Canada, my group fished, swam, ran, jacuzzied, and paddleboarded. With each group and each retreat, we got out of our comfort zones and our heads and became fully present in having fun. It was important for our creativity, brain function, relationships, and overall well-being to take the time out from the hard mental work to relax and enjoy life. We all were better for it, and it allowed us to be more productive with our work.

Just look at some of the headquarters of top companies such as Google and Facebook; their campuses look like a playground made of my childhood dreams. More and more corporations are recognizing the importance of play in building team culture.

Play is also why vacations are so enjoyable and refreshing. They are built around it! But how many of us actually use all of our vacation time? More often than not, I hear of people rolling over weeks and weeks of vacation every year. We need that vacation time to play, relax, be a kid, and mentally and physically recharge so we are ready to be our best self when we return.

Incorporating play into your life doesn't have to be

that difficult. Find a new hobby or passion. Play can be a physical activity, but it can also be a book club, a knitting circle, or rolling around on the floor with your children or pet. Whatever it may be, make sure you are doing it for your benefit and not to please someone else or because you feel an obligation. Play should always be fun and never feel forced.

Lesson one: Making time for play creates connection, increases creativity, and brightens your spirit.

FOCUS ON THE POSITIVE

Have you ever followed a toddler around for a day? Those of you who are parents are yelling at me right now, "Yeah, every damn day!" It's exhausting! I love how innocent and literal a young child can be. They take joy in the simplest things in life and focus on the positive instead of dwelling on the negative. That's a big lesson we can all learn.

Every summer, my extended family gathers at my aunt and uncle's cabin in northern Wisconsin for an annual family weekend. This past summer, my three-year-old nephew was running around outside with the dogs and ended up stepping in a bit of dog poop. As my sister was washing off the poop on one of his Crocs, one of my aunts said, "Oh no, buddy! You've got poop on your shoe!" He looked up, lifted his other foot, and said with the biggest smile on his face, "Yeah, but not on this one!" Then he ran away, one Croc on and one Croc off, unconcerned with the minor inconvenience. He got his other Croc back as soon as it was clean and went right back to running around with the dogs. No worse for the wear. I sat back and laughed.

an infinite love

My nephew immediately saw the positive in his situation, even when someone pointed out the negative. He also didn't let the negative set him back from his goals. He went right back to his activity. I know this is a bit of a stretch when compared to all the trials and tribulations of adulthood, but why does it have to be? Why can't we play life that simple?

When there is a hiccup or setback, find the positive, work around it, fix the situation, and then get right back up and proceed toward your goals. Wouldn't that make the outcome that much more rewarding? The pride and self-love you will demonstrate to yourself will be an even better reward. The feeling that no matter what the obstacle, you can accomplish your goals. Keep it positive, keep it simple.

Lesson two: Find the positive in negative situations.

BIRTHDAYS ARE THE BEST DAYS

I've realized in recent years how much I enjoy spending time with the toddlers in my life. I sit back and observe and try and place myself in their headspace, a.k.a. being present. Nothing matters to them except what they are doing at that exact moment, and if they don't like the present, they change it. Why is that so hard for adults to do? When do you unlearn this concept? Be in the present, enjoy the present, and if you don't, change the circumstances. So simple, so smart. Those toddlers, they're doing life right!

One of my best friends' little boy was turning two, and I wanted to stop by their house and bring a gift. I told my friend I was bringing a favorite treat of mine. My friend, who has the world's biggest sweet tooth, expected me to show up with some delectable sweet treat for his son. Which meant, as the parent, he got to enjoy about 90 percent of the treat. He was royally disappointed when I showed up with balloons. He said, "How am I supposed to enjoy balloons? I can't eat that. I thought you'd bring a sweet treat!" As we proceeded to have one of the most fun afternoons I've had in a long time, he was shocked to realize how sweet of a treat my balloons were after all.

The best part of the whole afternoon was watching his two-year-old son and how excited he got from the simple pleasure of playing with balloons. Some we blew up and batted around, some we purposely popped, and some we released around the room, creating that farting sound we all find funny no matter what age we are. Joe giggled and giggled. He couldn't get enough and ran from person to person, handing them balloons and saying, "Again, again!" We laughed and laughed. The afternoon was pure joy, seeing the pleasure and excitement on his face as we played with something as simple as balloons.

We then turned on some music and watched Joe unabashedly dance, dance, dance. He swayed his hips and snapped his fingers (or attempted to!), and the joy it brought was indescribable. Soon, he had us all up and dancing.

Bringing other people joy is one of the best feelings in the world. We need to do more of that. It's the best two-for-one deal around. One person brings joy, and two people are rewarded.

Lesson three: Being present in the moment brings joy and happiness.

an infinite love

DANCE YOUR DANCE

As we were busting our best moves to the music, I looked at little Joe and at the other adults in the room and thought, *When did we learn to stop dancing? When did we become self-conscious of what we look like when we dance, both literally and figuratively?*

My nickname in grad school was LBoogie because you could always find me on the dance floor. I was a dancer, and not one of those I-need-to-have-four-drinks-in-me-before-I-hit-the-dance-floor dancers. I had a routine. During undergrad, Abby—my partner in crime—and I would walk into the bar, find a guy to buy us a beer, and immediately do a hot lap to scope out the situation: who was there, where people were congregated, who was the best bet to buy us drinks all night, and most importantly, who was DJing. We had two objectives in mind: getting free drinks all night and getting our requests played. We weren't looking to hook up, and we weren't looking to make friends; we were looking to dance and dance to the songs we liked. We went straight to the dance floor and stayed there all night.

Many nights, we would hear people say, "Wow, the DJ is killing it tonight, jam after jam after jam," and we would nod, smile, and give ourselves a high-five because, well, mission accomplished. We would leave the bar soaked in sweat because we had just spent four hours dancing. Guys would try to dance with us or give us a hug but then turn around and walk away because we were so sweaty. They were grossed out, and we didn't care one bit. All we wanted to do was dance. Half our friends would say, "Were you at the bar? We didn't see you all night."

lisa beck

Well, if you didn't dance, chances were you wouldn't be seeing us.

Now, many years post-school, I can't remember the last time I danced like that. An occasional wedding here and there, I guess. I'm finding I don't have the opportunity and maybe the stamina to do a four-hour dance marathon, but I can do spontaneous dance breaks by myself or with my niece, nephew, and friends. It's important for us to get back to dancing like an uninhibited child.

If you're going to dance, you need some music. I have found that, often, one good jam can turn my mood right around. Music to me is a necessary function of life. I'll admit I don't attend many concerts, as seeing live music isn't really my thing, but I always have music playing at my house. I like to work out to music, walk to music, write to music, meditate to music, and clean my house to music. You name the occasion, and I can put together a playlist for it. I even have a playlist for self-love, which has all my favorite tunes, some attached to great memories and some that I just love no matter how many times I've heard them. You know those songs, the ones that never get old and you could listen to it a thousand times in a row and still want to listen a thousand more times.

Learn to dance your dance. When I was dancing, I didn't care what I looked like or who was looking at me. I was fully embracing the moment, had a mindful presence, and lost all self-consciousness. Take initiative to do this more in your life. Stop caring what other people are thinking, and dance your own dance. Love yourself enough to know the only opinion that matters is your own.

an infinite love

Lesson four: Embrace authenticity and self-happiness by dancing your own dance.

FROM ONE WEIRDO TO ANOTHER

Have you noticed that children are sometimes just plain weird? They say and do some of the strangest things. We may shake our heads, roll our eyes, and maybe muster a giggle, but we only love them more because of their weirdness. They are 100-percent authentic in who they are and never hide it. When I watch my niece wear a winter hat, sunglasses, Superman cape, and three-sizes-too-large rain boots bob and weave through the house muttering some gibberish about the stuffed unicorn she's dragging behind her, I can't help but think, *This girl is so beautifully, innocently weird. I wouldn't want her to be anyone else!*

Get OK with your weirdness. Walk in it and embrace your quirks. Everyone is unique. Everyone is weird in their own amazing way. My dad is one of the strangest, weirdest men I know. My sister, mom, and I will have open conversations about how weird he is. We just laugh and shake our heads. It's one of the qualities I love and admire most about him because he truly owns it. He radiates strength, calmness, and confidence in who he is, and we embrace all parts of him. He's never trying to please anyone but himself, and he will outright say, "I am who I am, and I'm sixty-nine years old . . . I'm not changing now." I accept that and wish others could see how awesome their weirdness truly is.

What is strange and maybe off-putting to one person is quirky and special to another. I went on a few dates with a guy who really surprised me. The more we chatted and I got to know him, the more I found myself adoring his personality. One day I asked him, "How are you still single? You're so great!" His response was, "Because I'm weird. Even my mom says I'm strange." I laughed and said, "Yeah, but that's the reason I like you! You aren't like me. Complete opposite, in fact." I found I truly liked him for who he was and respected the weirdness that made up his personality.

The other day, a friend gave me one of the best compliments I have ever received. I was telling him a story about wanting to write a children's book series about my puppy, Daks Barkington Fluffer Nutter, and he laughed and said I was so strange. He knows I love to give everyone, including animals, some pretty oddball nicknames. It's how I show love. At any rate, I loved that he thought I was odd. That meant I was being authentic and was embracing and loving all of me. People's quirks keep life interesting. Be you, be bright, be weird, and if someone doesn't appreciate your weirdness, keep walking. Trust me, there's someone right around the corner who will.

In the name of research, I reached out to my girl gang and asked them to tell me some of my quirks. The qualities that make them roll their eyes or giggle but love me anyway. At first, I thought maybe they didn't understand the question, as I found I received more compliments than quirks. But then I realized no, it wasn't them, it was me! I was looking for and expecting negative traits, like quirks were a bad thing. Turns out I was fully loving myself and embracing my quirks and seeing them as compliments because they are. They complement my personality and make me who I am. Don't wait for someone else's permission to

an infinite love

be your authentic self. You don't need anyone's approval but your own. Your unique qualities make you exactly who you are and what the world needs to see. Your gifts and the way you see the world are unique. Your friends appreciate that about you; otherwise they wouldn't choose to be your friends. You be you, and go forth with all the confidence of a naked two-year-old running amok!

Lesson five: Embrace your quirks, because they lead to a more self-fulfilled and authentic life.

CALL TO ACTION

Play more! Define what play means to you and how you can add more of it in your life.

Make an effort to be fully present with whatever activity you are doing.

List some of your own quirks and how you can embrace them.

Create a playlist for any time you need a little self-love — just press play, and don't forget to dance!

CHAPTER FOUR

The Pursuit of Happiness Is an Inside Job

"Happiness is a choice, not a result. Nothing will make you happy until you choose to be happy. No person will make you happy unless you decide to be happy. Your happiness will not come to you. It can only come from you."

—Ralph Marston

I woke up really happy today. Happy with what I accomplished last week. Happy that it is a Monday and I get the opportunity to tackle another week. Happy that somehow one of my gifts is being a world-class multitasker and that the more I have going on, the more productive I am. I felt genuinely content and extremely happy.

Normally, I'd celebrate this feeling, but today I was feeling guilty. See, my aunt, whom I am particularly close with, passed suddenly last night. Even as my mom told me the news, I couldn't shake the contentment and happiness from my soul. I asked myself, *Why am I feeling this way? I should be crying right now. My whole family is devastated at the loss of one of our own.* Then it dawned on me that I was so happy because that was my aunt's message to me. She was content and happy and wanted me to know. I could feel her energy around and within me. I recognized that the tears would come, as she will be deeply missed, but for now I remain happy because I know that's how she wants me to feel, and it's how my soul feels deep within.

I also know it's been a journey to get here. Sure, I've been happy before—many times, in fact—but I've never been as sure and filled with such internal happiness as I have been ever since I made the choice to do so. In my choosing to be happy, I had to look at when I wasn't happy and recognize the emotions behind those feelings. Only then was I able to accept myself and welcome true happiness into my life.

WHEN THE DREAM ISN'T REALITY

Have you ever met someone and immediately felt like you've known each other forever? You just click and are instantly family. You fall into these roles with one another that feel entirely new yet also so familiar. I met Carrie the summer between my junior and senior years of college. A friend and I were athletic training interns at a hockey camp, and at the time Carrie was dating the owner's son. The following summer, my friend and I were back for another round of broken wrists, stitches, poison ivy, and pucks to the face. As we got out of our cars on the first day of staff check-in, Carrie saw us from afar and yelled across campus, "They let you bi-otches back!" Obviously,

an infinite love

my response to her welcoming hello was sharp, witty, and perfectly timed: "You know you missed us!" Thus was the beginning of a never-wavering soul-sister friendship.

A few years later, when I was twenty-four—master's degree completed, internships done, and jobless—Carrie said, "Come back to Minnesota and live with us. Work at the hockey camp for the summer, and we will find you a job." Well, summer turned into fall and fall into winter. We spent many, many cold winter days and nights drinking wine and watching reality TV on her couch, laughing our asses off and simultaneously crying our eyes out.

Ultimately, we were both feeling a little stuck, unhappy, and lost in our current positions in life. Me especially. She's the one who pushed me to get out of the small town, keep putting myself out there, and move forward with my dreams, always reassuring me she had my back. I still didn't know exactly what I wanted to do with my life, but I knew she was right.

The tricky thing about being in your midtwenties is you feel like you are a full-blown adult but realize quickly that sometimes adulting is a false advertisement.

I found this time in my life to be more difficult than I ever expected. I was a smart, hardworking woman with my master's degree . . . Where were all the jobs? I had this idea that once I finished my master's degree, the job, the house, my happiness, and the plan would be handed to me on a silver platter. When that didn't happen (shocker), I didn't know what to do. I wasn't afraid of working and took whatever jobs came to me, but I wasn't making the kind of money I expected or following the life path I had anticipated.

lisa beck

Some of my friends were in the same position as me, but many were getting kick-ass jobs, buying houses, getting married, and living a much more financially free life than I was. I really struggled with this and with my self-worth, which was pretty much nonexistent at that time in my life. I gained weight and wasn't happy where I was. The problem was that I placed my happiness in the hands of others and external circumstances. Instead of being happy for my successful friends and honoring all their hard work and their journeys, I found myself getting jealous and depressed and slowly shying away socially. I couldn't see all the good I was doing, all the lessons I was learning, all the times I was a great friend lending an ear or a hand to hold. I couldn't see the opportunities and great things coming my way.

The story I was telling myself was that I wasn't good enough for them and that things would have been better if only I had made different choices. *Why did I choose the career path I did? Why didn't I do this better? If only I went there, chose that* . . . if only, if only, if only. These were the questions on continual repeat in my mind. Looking back, I now recognize the pressure I put on myself got so bad that it caused an anxiety attack the day my younger sister graduated from college. I'm the older sibling; I'm supposed to lead the way. First one up the mountain and all that. I was the first one up the mountain, but it turns out that we took two totally different paths.

I'm so lucky to have the people I have in my life because they pushed me and opened my eyes to the wealth I have inside me. It took me a while to stop telling myself the same sad poor-me story, stop being jealous of other

an infinite love

people's journeys, and start honoring my own. By honoring my own journey, I was able to feel the happiness inside of me.

Lesson one: Honoring your own journey leads to internal happiness

HI! MY NAME'S JENNY

If people who have suffered tremendous tragedy in their lives can find a way to honor and love themselves enough to exude happiness, then we all can. As I was navigating my way out of my depressed, anxiety-ridden, overpressured state and working on more mindful happiness, I was reminded of my friend Jenny. I met Jenny in grad school. I moved from Minnesota to Massachusetts because I had always had an inkling that I'd like to live out East and thought, *Why not now?* I looked up a few schools that had the master's program I was interested in, pulled out a map, closed my eyes, pointed to a dot, and let fate do the talking. I was going to apply to whatever school was closest to where my finger landed.

As I entered my first class, I noticed this girl in the back of the room. She looked nice and had a warm, welcoming, and infectious smile. We introduced ourselves, and when she heard my accent, she asked where I was from. I didn't think I had much of a Minnesotan accent, but my East Coast friends begged to differ. I mentioned I needed some school supplies, and she told me she was local and offered to show me around and take me shopping. Jenny proceeded to invite me to dinner that weekend at her mom's house. We had just met, and already she was opening up not only herself but her home and entire family to a perfect stranger! I went to Sunday dinner and met her grandparents, aunts, uncles, brothers, neighbors, and a random friend who stopped by. Who was this girl . . . and this family? This lovely family that welcomed me as one of their own and was excited to learn about me and where I was from. They were all so nice, welcoming, and happy.

When Jenny was in junior high, one of her older brothers became sick and passed away. Six months later, in the midst of grieving the loss of her brother, her father unexpectedly passed as well. How can a family that has suffered such loss be so welcoming and so happy? I asked Jenny this, and she said it was because her mom gave them no other choice. They must choose happiness at any cost. It's important to recognize that happiness is a choice. It can be hard work at times, but it is a choice you must make in an effort to love yourself more and live a full, vivacious life. Jenny and the rest of her family are shining examples!

Lesson two: Internal happiness is a choice. No one can choose it but you.

CELEBRATE THE HAPPINESS OF OTHERS

We've all been there. You hear about a friend, coworker, family member, or random stranger getting a promotion, getting engaged, getting pregnant, buying a house, winning the lottery . . . whatever it may be. You put a smile on your face and act so happy for them, and maybe you are, but inside it's a battle—a battle of happiness and jealousy, of *congrats* and *why not me*, of *we should celebrate* and *I want to curl up in a ball on my couch and not see anyone ever.* When

an infinite love

I started focusing on my own self-care, my own self-love, finding my purpose and passions, choosing my own happiness, that all changed. I found myself being happy for and celebrating other people's victories. Their happiness exemplified my own happiness.

Case in point: A friend of mine made the men's Canadian Olympic hockey team. When I found out, I started crying because I was so genuinely proud of him and his hard work. I knew how proud his older brother, my dearest friend, was feeling, and I couldn't help but share in that sentiment. All his hard work, dedication, and time and the fact it couldn't have happened to a more genuine guy made me so proud and so happy. Now I find I rarely become jealous, just proud, happy, and a bit emotional when people I love succeed. I will be the first one giving a smile, offering a high five, and cheering them on.

Be happy and excited about who you are and the journey you are on. Honor others and their journeys. When and if jealousy shows up, remember you never know the story someone is telling themself. You never know the struggles they went through. Life is hard. Learn from the lessons, and celebrate what you have learned. Be there for others, but more importantly be there for yourself.

When you take the time to appreciate yourself and your accomplishments, you naturally start to appreciate and want to celebrate the accomplishments of others. The relationship you have with yourself sets the stage for every other relationship. Above all else, love yourself the most and it will lead you to enduring happiness for yourself and others.

lisa beck

Lesson three: Working on your own happiness allows you to be happy for others.

HAPPINESS SURROUNDS YOU EVERY DAY
Do you ever have a moment where you stop and think, *Wow . . . I'm really happy right now!* What are you doing during these moments? For me, this thought tends to come at three different points.

1. When I'm sitting around with my loved ones, be it friends or family, and we are laughing our asses off at an old memory, something that was said or done, or a general topic at hand. Like crying, may-have-piddled-in-my-pants laughing. I smile now just thinking about it. There are different groups of people and different memories, but all bring me extreme joy.
2. When I honor my true self and do more of what my soul loves. My soul loves snuggling with my puppy, being in the mountains and travel in general, the sun on my face, massages, warm coffee, delicious meals, bringing joy to others, writing, playing, and the feeling of completing a really hard workout. It also really, really loves growth and passion, both in myself and in helping others.
3. When I'm walking. I walk a lot. When it gets nice out, I'm out the door and walking. Sometimes a quick twenty minutes, other times an hour and a half. I love to look at the curb appeal of houses and think about what I would do if I lived there. I'm typically listening to music or a podcast. More often than not, my mind wanders and I think—about everything. I tune into

an infinite love

nature and tune out the problems in my world. Many times, I find myself smiling and think, *I'm so damn happy right now.* Happy with my life, where I am in this moment, and where I'm headed. I don't know where my path is leading, but I am happy and content in the moment and have the faith in my journey to know it leads to more happiness.

Lesson four: External factors do not lead to long-term happiness, but they can enhance it.

CALL TO ACTION

Journal about your happiest times.
- Where are you?
- What are you doing?
- Who are you with?
- How can you add more of this in your life?

Reflect and write about a time you became jealous or angry because of someone else's happiness.
- Ask yourself what fears are behind these emotions.
- How can you choose happiness instead?

Create an emergency happiness protocol. Find one or two simple things that will brighten your day when you find yourself down in the dumps.

Think about your own awesome accomplishments.

Do something that celebrates yourself.

CHAPTER FIVE

Find Your Mantra

"A Mantra is nothing more than a collection of words strung together to create a positive effect."
—Robin Sharma

Scholars believe mantras date back as far as 1000 BC, with the literal meaning of the Sanskrit word being "instruments of thought." These instruments of thought can be found throughout many world religions and different schools of philosophy but can also be found on posters, living-room walls, and sports teams' locker rooms. No matter where they appear, mantras are meant to be repeated and evoke a feeling of belief, setting your mind on a clear and conscious course.

LET IT BE GREAT!
A good friend of mine uses the phrase "Let it be great!" on a daily basis. He has it posted on a sign at home and at the office. When he isn't particularly looking forward to a social engagement, has a big meeting, or is feeling a

bit anxious about a situation, he repeats these words and knows all will be fine.

Most colleges and universities and even branches of the military have mantras. My alma mater had written "Through these doors walk champions" above the doorway between the locker room and the hockey rink. Mantras help get your mind in the present and can make goals and tasks easier to accomplish. When it comes to mantras, there are no specific rules. They can change with your day, thoughts, mood, and life as long as they promote positivity and elicit strong beliefs.

Find areas in your daily life where you want to invoke an inner strength and belief. Find words that help you do so. Repeat this phrase as many times as necessary for you to go forward with courage, grace, and unwavering confidence in yourself.

Lesson one: A mantra can create unity, clarify a goal, set precedence, provide comfort, and set an intention.

MEDITATION, MANTRAS, AND THE MIND-BODY CONNECTION

Research has proven that meditation reduces stress levels, which in turn can reduce symptoms of stress-related conditions. Meditation has also been proven to lower anxiety and depression, promote emotional health, aid in sleep, enhance self-esteem, and positively affect mental health.

Yongey Mingyur Rinpoche, a Buddhist monk and a mindfulness meditation prodigy, let scientists study his brain activity during meditation. After asking Rinpoche to cultivate a sense of compassion throughout his meditation, scientists found the activity in the part of his brain

an infinite love

that measured empathy shot up 700–800 percent. Scientists had never seen someone display such a controlled increase in brain activity. They also noticed that even though Yongey Mingyur Rinpoche was forty-one years old, he had the brain of a thirty-three-year-old.

I try to find time to meditate every day. I'm not perfect by any means, but it's called a meditation *practice*, right? For me, walking meditation feels the best. The feel of the wind blowing in the trees, the sound of the birds chirping, and the warm sun beating down on my skin make me happy. I am pretty high-energy and have found a meditation practice really grounds me. I always get a sense of calm, connectedness, and being fully present after I meditate. Any thoughts of stress or anxiety seem to float away.

Sometimes I repeat a mantra throughout my meditation practice. Most of the time it is "I am love and light," reminding myself to spread love and positivity. Other days, it depends on what I am looking to focus on. Lots of times I use a gratitude mantra and list something I am grateful for with every breath. Some days it's focused on money, why I love it, and what it can bring into my life. Everything is energy, and if I can raise my vibration to attract more love, light, gratefulness, money, and so on into my life, then I'm going to repeat these words every damn day!

Like anything, the more you practice meditation, the easier it gets. I started small. I set a timer for one minute and practiced sitting still and focusing on deep breathing and a mantra or value word the entire minute. Gradually, one minute turned into two, then five and ten. Now my seated practice is fifteen to thirty minutes and my walking practice can be the entire length of my walk.

There are many different ways one can practice meditation. Stereotypically, we think of sitting cross-legged on the floor "OM-ing" our way to enlightenment. If I'm being honest, when I first started, this didn't work for me. I found I had too much energy and needed to move. I started walking and listening to a guided meditation, but even with that assistance, sometimes it was still not quite right for me. I played around with many different variations and found that if I listened to light music or instrumentals, walked at my own pace, and focused on the world around me and the path directly in front of me, I easily got into a nice flow.

There are various free apps, videos, and links to help you start a meditation practice, and many offer meditations on anything you can think of. Your mind may wander, and that is perfectly fine; catch yourself and bring it back to stillness. Try not to think, just be. I find this is where a mantra becomes handy. When I focus on that word or saying, my mind is less apt to wander.

Some find it helps to create a ritual or routine around their meditation practice. Same time, same place, light candles, set-the-mood kind of thing. If you ride the bus or train to work, that is a great time to practice a meditation. If you find you are like me and need some movement with your practice, try a restorative or lower-intensity yoga class. Qigong is also an option. Doesn't matter how you choose to meditate, just start and notice the benefits it brings into your life.

Meditation can help you control your relationship

an infinite love

with your emotions. Instead of reacting to fear, anxiety, depression, stress, or other problems, you can inwardly observe your emotions without engaging with them. You need to train your mind just as you would train your body.

Lesson two: Practicing meditation can strengthen the mind-body connection and can bring focus to your life.

WELCOME TO VALUE WORK . . . MAY I TAKE YOUR ORDER?

Value words are great to incorporate into mantras. How often in our lives do we actually sit down and think about what our values are, why these values ring true to us, and how we use them in our daily decisions and actions?

Over the course of the past two years, I have gotten into leadership coaching. I've worked with women, men, small businesses, and high school coaches and teams. One activity I've come to really enjoy in both my training and in the course of my coaching is value work. When I was attending a leadership retreat in Kenora, Canada, on the beautiful shores of Lake of the Woods, we did value work for about two days straight. We had value words coming out of our ears, to the point where many of them were just becoming sounds with no meaning attached. Our job was to whittle two days' worth of value words into fourteen words, which would then be whittled down to about eight or nine or so. Are you kidding me?! I had about a hundred words written in front of me, and each held meaning to me. I'm not good with these types of decisions! Although I absolutely loved it, this entire process was difficult for me. At the end of the day, my brain hurt and I was exhausted.

Many of our values are taught to us by our parents

and theirs from their parents, and so on up the generational ladder. When I think of the values that my parents taught me, I think of respect, kindness, and hard work.

What values did your parents and grandparents pass along to you? Do you still adhere to these values, or do you find yourself shifting away? It's important to find what feels true to you and to honor your own truth and nobody else's.

Also look at your close circle and mentors in your life and note the values you honor in them and why. Do you aspire to obtain these values? Do you share a lot of the same values? Do they honor and respect your values?

There's nothing wrong with values changing as your life and circumstances change. That's one of our greatest gifts. We always have a choice. It may not be easy, it may not come lightly, and it may not be for the benefit of all, but we always have a choice.

I believe it's also important to write down each role you play in life. For instance, I'm a business owner, sister, daughter, niece, aunt, friend, leader, speaker, writer, and so on. Ask yourself, *What do I value in each of these roles, and does it differ from role to role? How do I want to be seen in each role? What message am I trying to communicate?* Clear values help to establish clearer missions and vision for your life. People will only treat you as well as you treat yourself. If you don't honor your own value system, you can't expect others to either.

Lesson three: Defining the values you assign to different roles you play in life helps to give direction, create boundaries, and establish self-worth.

CALL TO ACTION

Start a meditation practice.

Create your own mantra.
- Where in your life can you use a little positive encouragement?

Make a list of all the roles you play in life. Assign a value to each of these roles then ask yourself the following questions:
- How do I want to be seen in each role?
- What does each role mean to me?
- Am I living up to my own values?
- Are other people honoring me and my values?
- What changes need to be made so I can say yes to the last two questions?

CHAPTER SIX

Body Love

"It's also helpful to realize that this very body that we have, that's sitting right here right now . . . with its aches and its pleasures . . . is exactly what we need to be fully human, fully awake, fully alive."

—Pema Chödrön

Having infinite love for yourself means loving all of you, inside and out, head to toe, exactly where you are. Loving your big heart, your adventurous spirit, your quiet nature, your humor, or your intelligence can be easy. But loving your body—the love handles, cellulite, goofy toes, or misshapen breasts—can be trickier. It's important that we honor compassion, forgiveness, and even humor to accept ourselves, small earlobes and all, exactly as we are.

I WON'T BE HANDCUFFED TO MY DISEASE

When I was eleven years old, my parents noticed I was drastically losing weight and going to the bathroom *a lot*. They knew this wasn't normal and brought me to the doctor. I was then diagnosed with type 1 diabetes, an autoim-

an infinite love

mune condition where one's own immune system attacks the beta cells in the pancreas, stopping the pancreas from producing the hormone insulin. This results in too much sugar in the blood—not a good thing.

At the time, I really had no idea what diabetes was, what it entailed, or how life-changing it would be for me. It's funny what we remember; the day I was diagnosed, I had Oreos for a snack in school, and I thought I'd never be able to have Oreos again (not true). My family and I embraced this new challenge as best we could and tried to welcome our new normal. My mom was beyond amazing and started a local support group for families dealing with juvenile diabetes. I know it was her way to build community to help her heal, deal, and learn so she could be the best support for me. Although she's not still involved, I'm proud to say the support group continues to this day. Go Mom!!

We didn't let this disease hold us back one bit. As a unit we said, "OK, what's next?" My parents made sure, even at my young age, to preach to me that I should not let the disease control me but that I should learn to control it. They gave me the freedom to be a kid and the independence to handle things on my own, in my own way, all the while keeping a watchful eye and a supportive hand when I needed it.

Our small school held dances nearly every Friday as fundraisers for a sports team or organizations. On one particular Friday night when I was thirteen, I went to the bathroom to give myself an insulin injection, and a chaperone walked in and saw me. I could see the look of panic on her face as she quickly turned around and left. When

I left the bathroom, two policemen were waiting for me. I quickly realized she made the assumption I was shooting up with heroin. Let me tell you, two policemen escorting a scrawny, geeky girl out of a school dance can draw quite the attention. Attention I did not want. At thirteen, all I wanted was to fit in, and I could hear the rumors starting to snowball throughout the student body. I was embarrassed to have all this unwanted attention on me for something I had no control over. I was angry at the chaperone for jumping to a ridiculous conclusion without talking to me and even angrier at my body and this stupid disease. For many years, I was ashamed and didn't want anyone to know I have diabetes. I didn't want to stand out or be labeled as weird. I also knew how ridiculous this thinking was, and I was even more ashamed of that. It was a vicious cycle.

Slowly, I grew and learned to love my body for all the wonderful things it could do. My drive, my ability to think positive and overcome obstacles, my consistent workout schedule, and my healthy diet all came along because I have diabetes, and for this I am grateful.

Lesson one: Love your body exactly where it's at. Forgive yourself. Find something body-positive to acknowledge and celebrate.

WHEN YOU TRY, YOU MUST TRUST

When I started volunteering with a local nonprofit that created programs for young adults with developmental disabilities, I helped to create a program called Move and Groove. It was our goal to get our members active, challenging our bodies, while grooving to music.

an infinite love

Our members had varying levels of physical and mental disabilities. What I absolutely loved most about this group was their willingness to try anything I put in front of them. Whatever stage they were in physically, we would challenge their bodies and they would always step up to the plate. Many would have a look of fear and trepidation at the task ahead of them, as they didn't have the body control we did and each exercise required a lot of trust. A trust of the body, trust of movement, and trust in the person assisting.

Through the help of other members, aides, and family members, everyone attempted each task, and as we practiced and challenged their bodies, we could physically see the mind-body connection click and their confidence skyrocket. It was the absolute best, and many days brought tears to my eyes. We failed lots but always picked ourselves back up through the help and support of others and were sure to celebrate every victory.

My love and admiration for the members and their own uniqueness will never waiver. I am forever changed and forever in awe.

Lesson two: Trust in your body's capabilities and challenge yourself. Let your perceived flaws become part of your uniqueness.

BE YOUR OWN HEALTH ADVOCATE

A majority of the population I work with in the health and wellness industry are people with chronic conditions and post-surgery. I help get them up, moving, and exercising, guided by the protocols set forth by their doctors, physical therapists, and any other practitioner involved. Over the years, I have become a central cog in their health and wellness journey, communicating with various practitioners, offering suggestions for possible alternative health-care practices, teaching them about the mind-body connection, and pushing them forward, all the while letting their body be our guide. I always remind them, "I am on your side and will do my best to be of service to you, but *you* are your own health advocate!" Never be afraid to question a practitioner or therapist. Seek a second opinion if needed. You are the one in charge of you! Only you know what you see, feel, and experience.

In my own life, I practice this regularly. The work I do on my body is continual, from my sometimes sluggish metabolism to my pretty consistent digestive issues. I've tried every diet under the sun and have seen every type of practitioner, both conventional and alternative. Only through trial and error, lots of questions, discipline (something I can struggle with), and patience have I managed to get a handle on what my body needs to feel and work its best. My body loves short, hard workouts. Working with weights grounds me. What my body loves most is when I dedicate time to stretch and foam roll. That's when I feel most connected to my body, and I swear I can hear my body saying thank you.

Your body will tell you exactly what it needs to thrive and survive. It is up to you to listen. Be sure to listen with compassion and kindness. Use these experiences to learn and grow. Make any necessary changes, and know that body love is a practice that grows stronger with time and effort.

Lesson three: Listen to your body and treat it with kindness.

an infinite love

YOU ARE WHAT YOU EAT

There are many nutritional plans available to us, with scientific data to back up each one. Find a healthy way of eating that works for you. Think of food as fuel for your brain, muscles, and other systems. Many people don't recognize that food is also a big factor in our recovery. Whether you are an everyday athlete or weekend warrior, healthy food assists in the repair of tissues so you can continue to participate in your activities. It's imperative that you fuel your engine with high-quality foods. Fresh, natural, and organic are always better than processed. Eating high-quality foods has a huge impact by affecting our moods, increasing energy levels, and sharpening cognitive function.

Feeling bloated, sluggish, exhausted, or foggy and having headaches, stomachaches, frequent injuries, loose stools, or constipation are all not normal and all point to possible digestive issues. Our gut is considered our second brain and the start of our immune system. If we don't take care of this, all systems can go awry. You know the saying "Listen to your gut"? Do it! It will talk to you loud and clear; it is up to you to listen.

Lesson four: Eating healthy is honoring your body and showing yourself infinite love

MOVE IT OR LOSE IT, BABY

As a society, we sit a lot. In our cars, at work, at home on the couch. But you have to get up and get moving. It's important that you find a workout routine that works for you. With today's technology, we have access to all sorts of fitness and workout routines for all ages and levels.

lisa beck

There's literally no excuse for not working out. Listen to your body and be patient, smart, and kind.

Working out should not be a form of punishment. I know way too many people that kill themselves with each and every workout. If they don't puke, it doesn't count. We've all heard the phrase "No pain, no gain." I strongly dislike this phrase. For them, exercise is a form of punishment from choices they made in the recent or not-so-recent past. This is not a healthy mindset and is absolutely not showing their body love. There is a big difference in pushing yourself during your workouts and punishing yourself.

If you have a mentally or emotionally stressful day, adding on a physically demanding workout is just adding to the stress, not helping to dissipate it. Be mindful of this, and choose a less physically demanding workout or complete rest. Rest is just as important as the workout. Often I see someone's body continue to break down because they ignore the stressors and continue to push. They wonder why they are always having aches, pains, and injuries, yet they seem to refuse to listen to the signs their body is giving them.

Lesson five: Showing your body love is moving your body by exercising in a healthy way.

EXPLORE YOUR BODY

So often we have such shame, disgust, and overall icky feelings toward our body. We refuse to even look at ourselves in the mirror. If we do, all we see are flaws. They are the first thing we focus on and the first thing we pick out in pictures. My challenge to you is this: the next time

an infinite love

you look at a picture of yourself or see yourself naked, point out one or two positives. Focus on the positives.

Stand naked in the mirror and look at yourself. Take your time and really look. It's important for our health to know what our body looks like. Ask yourself, *Is that spot always there or is that new? Where did I get that bruise? Is my posture different?* Move your body around. How does that feel? What do you notice? Does everything feel normal, or do you feel stiff and tight in some areas? Notice the signs that you need to show our body more love.

Look at your sex organs. What do they look like? Every person's is unique, so get to know your own. There is no shame in exploring your own body. How can you tell if something isn't normal if you don't know what your sex organs look like in the first place? We are taught at such a young age to suppress anything sexual. This includes the act, the feelings, and the parts. We need to do the exact opposite and talk more about it. We need to get rid of the shame and stigma and do more educating. I love how open and honest and full of curiosity little kids are when it comes to their body parts. I remember when I was around twelve and my cousin was three, she came running down the stairs saying, "Guess what, Lisa? Boys have a penis and girls have a vagina. I have a vagina!" She giggled. "Boys pee from the outside and I pee from the inside!" We should all be that proud and nonchalant.

Lesson six: Show your body love by exploring all its parts.

CALL TO ACTION

Create five to ten body-positive affirmations. Write or read them out loud every day.

Dedicate thirty minutes of your day to movement or exercise.

Dedicate time to meal prep so you eat healthy during the week.

When grocery shopping, stick to the perimeter of the store, where most of the fresh food is found.

Set aside some time to get to know and explore your own body.

CHAPTER SEVEN

Building or Unbuilding a Routine

"It's a hard thing to leave any deeply routine life, even if you hate it."

—John Steinbeck

Chatting on the phone one day after I got back from my Purpose and Passion leadership retreat in Costa Rica, my friend Colby and I started talking about life's purpose and passions. I credit him with part of the idea for this book. He was the one to awaken in me the concept that it doesn't matter who we are with, what we do, or where we live; if we aren't happy with ourselves, nothing else will be fulfilled.

During this phone conversation, we got into a discussion about routine. In general, we both agreed that routine is death. I'm not talking about the simple steps that people can take to set themselves up for success; I'm talking about the routine of life that people seem to get caught in. The resistance to change! We get in a rut, get up, do the thing, be the person, come home, go to bed, start all over. Before we realize it, we feel stuck, uninspired, sad, unmotivated, or even just plain unhappy. Maybe we don't even feel anything at all, and that's probably the worst feeling to have, just numb to life.

STAGNATION IS NOT A PERMANENT VACATION

I was in my midthirties, having worked long enough in my field to have established credibility, retirement accounts making money, and passport pages being filled, yet I was uninspired, stuck, and unhappy. Without recognizing it, as I believe happens to many of us, I was in a routine that wasn't fulfilling anymore. I was just living day to day.

We've all heard it a million times, but it's true: the best things, jobs, loves, and lives come from taking a risk. It comes from getting out of your own way, your comfort zone, and your routine. Find in your own life what areas need to change.

Embrace the change, lean into the change, hustle harder, and believe in yourself. Staying stuck in your routine is purely based out of fear, whether that's fear of the unknown, abandonment, judgment, or failure. We've all known failure at some point in our lives. We've got to get past the fear and jump in. If we fail, we get back up and try again. After all, that's how we all learned to walk. And look at what we can accomplish now just from the simple act of picking ourselves back up when we have fallen down.

Lesson one: Being stagnant doesn't lead to bliss. Step into fear and embrace the unknown.

an infinite love

UNHEALTHY ROUTINES

I have many healthy routines. I work out or move my body most days a week. I regularly get eight hours of sleep. I am a healthy eater, don't smoke, and seem to drink alcohol less and less as time goes on. I am structured and organized, following necessary protocols when it comes to working with my clients.

However, I came across one very unhealthy routine in my life: my actual lack of routine in my day-to-day! I am a free spirit, and as blessed as I am to work for myself and cultivate my own schedule, I've noticed too much freedom and a lack of discipline can lead me to an unproductive day. I can easily get distracted by bright, shiny objects and neglect adult responsibilities or, worse, stop making progress toward my goals.

Many of the most successful entrepreneurs, lifestylists, and thought leaders say a productive morning routine is the key to success. They advise us to get up at five o'clock and begin our day. Exercising, meditating, journaling, and eating a healthy breakfast all seem to be common threads in how to start your morning off on the right foot. I don't disagree with any of those concepts — and, in fact, I complete each of those tasks each day — but I admit, I struggle to get up before the sun rises. I've set the alarm for five or five thirty with the sole intention of starting my day as the thought leaders suggest, but for some reason I struggle to stick to it. Although I 100-percent agree with their concept, I think we need to figure out what works best for us and our daily life. Maybe the only time you have to yourself is at five thirty in the morning; if so, godspeed in your endeavors. But for me, at this time, that does not work.

lisa beck

Consistency is my sole downfall. I used to wake up and work with clients starting at five thirty every day, but when that changed, somehow waking up to work on myself at five thirty every day didn't go very well. I was showing up for everyone else but not willing to show up for myself. You are who you hang around with, so if you are a disciplined and consistent person, I invite you to join my inner circle. I will never lose my free spirit, as she's part of me, but I can learn to love and welcome more consistency in my life, as I know it ultimately leads to happiness.

My own lack of routine has become an unhealthy routine for me. What routines in your life have taken you down an unhealthy route? It doesn't have to be a physical act; an unhealthy routine can be something as simple as negative self-talk or emotions that crop up every time you see, hear, or experience something that triggers you. Or it might be pressing pause on life or ignoring feelings, responsibilities, chances, or opportunities and just zoning out.

Lesson two: Showing yourself love is recognizing and breaking free of unhealthy routines.

DON'T PRESS PAUSE

What is your security blanket when life gets hard, overwhelming, messy, stressful, or frightening? Mine is TV. I grab a blanket and some tea and zone out. I can zone out for a whole day if I want. When I do this, I am actively choosing not to deal with life and pushing pause. At one point I even cut off my cable to try to prevent some of this, but alas . . . damn you, Netflix!

an infinite love

I was finding ways to ignore this responsibility to myself—which is ironic because being responsible for ourselves is one of our biggest jobs in life. I recently got a puppy so I could care and be responsible for something else. This decision really helped me. The pup also helped me create more of a daily routine and accountability on the days I didn't feel like working out because I knew I would always get a thirty-minute walk in.

Why was I pushing pause on life? What was I purposely choosing to not deal with? It's funny how we can make a conscious decision for unconscious reasons. I chose to zone out because, at the time, my work wasn't lighting me up. I wasn't internally happy. I was suffering from burnout. The Universe was bringing me many opportunities, and many times I chose self-sabotage by not taking advantage and just staying in the easy path. I pushed pause on life because of perfectionism and fear of the unknown and hard work. The funny thing is, when I'm in the thick of something, I'm not afraid of hard work—in fact, I can be one of the hardest workers ever. Yet the thought of stepping out of this lane and taking a hard left turn into unknown territory was overwhelming, so instead of welcoming the challenge, hustling harder, and finding happiness knowing I was working toward something greater, I chose to press pause on life.

Part of learning to press play on life for me was building not only a daily routine but a routine that brings joy and ritual. If I am home in the morning, it's thirty minutes to myself journaling, meditating, or writing as I sip coffee. Then midmorning includes a thirty-minute walk with the dog as I listen to a podcast or uplifting music. I look forward to this time each day and find that I feel more accomplished and am happier as I continue throughout the day. Building in time for myself was essential in order for me to give back to others.

Lesson three: Don't pause your life. Creating rituals around a routine can bring joy and help to get you unstuck.

SET YOURSELF UP FOR SUCCESS

One of the people I met during my leadership retreat in Canada lives in British Columbia and works in a field similar to mine. We are both working on creating and building our own company and decided to hold each other accountable to our written vision and mission statements. Every other week—same day, same time—we talk. We make a concerted effort to stay in touch and help each other grow and reach our goals. We both listen and provide or seek advice as needed. I walk away from each conversation energized and motivated to keep on my mission, and I know she feels the same. What started out as a bimonthly conversation for accountability purposes has turned into a lasting friendship helping each of us to continue to grow in life. Finding an accountability partner who was in the trenches with me was a game changer.

Besides chatting with Allison, my accountability partner, once a month, I schedule a phone call with my mentor, Kathy. She was one of our coaches during my Canadian retreat and has been a leadership coach for many years. Her knowledge and experience in the leadership realm is essential to my growth and development. She oftentimes asks the hard questions.

an infinite love

As a mentor, she pushes me to think, expand beyond my limitations, and be a better version of myself. I look to her as an example of how I want to coach others. Careers shouldn't be a competition. The only one you should compete against is yourself. There is so much to learn from those that have had success. Just like in sports, teams always seem to play better when playing tougher competition. The wins are that much sweeter. Whether you want to be better in your field, a better mom, a better friend, or better at a particular skill or just need some accountability, find someone who can help you accomplish that. Find someone who will push and guide you.

Lesson four: Finding an accountability partner or mentor is crucial for accomplishing goals and growth.

CALL TO ACTION

List any routines in your life that are unhealthy or need to be changed.
- What is one thing you can do today to break this routine?

Find an accountability partner to help you accomplish your goals. Ask yourself the following questions:
- Will we meet in person, online, or via phone?
- How often will we meet?
- What do I want to get out of this relationship?

List or reflect on any areas in your life where you may be pressing pause or holding back.
- What are you pressing pause from?
- What do you do to press pause? Start to recognize these actions so you can catch yourself.
- What steps can you take to start playing bigger and challenge yourself more so you learn and grow?

List any areas in your life in which you need to find a bit more routine. Take the following questions into consideration:
- Can you build a ritual around this routine to help keep you consistent?

an infinite love

- Does this routine bring you joy? Can you find a routine that brings you joy and happiness?
- Write down what a happiness routine would look like.
- What does your perfect day look like?
- What is one thing you can do today to bring yourself closer to your happiness routine or perfect day?

CHAPTER EIGHT

Find Your Passion

"There is no passion to be found playing small—
in settling for a life that is less than the one you
are capable of living."

—Nelson Mandela

What's your passion? What lights your fire? What are you drawn to that brings you joy no matter what? Good days or bad days, you always come back for more. Do more of that, be more of that, and most importantly, make time for more of that. Let's all try to live our passion. Wouldn't that increase our overall happiness? I'm down!

I believe the people in your life should honor your passion. If something lights you up, makes you smile from ear to ear, gives you energy, and humbles you at times, why wouldn't others be happy for you and encourage you to follow your passion? Now, I know there may need to be structure and boundaries around certain passions. Unfortunately, adult responsibilities do come first, but after that, find a way to make it work.

Pursue your passion with vigor. Don't let anything

an infinite love

stop you or get in your way — especially yourself and the words "I can't." Pursing your passion will lead to overall happiness. I promise!

GIVE YOUR GIFTS

Can't seem to pinpoint a passion of yours? Ask yourself what gifts you have to offer the world. What are you good at? What do you enjoy doing for yourself or others? Find your gifts, find your passion. Spread it like wildfire! Whatever lights you up, do that. Share it — with friends, family, neighbors, and strangers. How does it make you feel to share something you're good at with others? Feels amazing, right? Don't you dare say, "But I don't have any gifts!" Yes, you do.

I have a family member who makes a playlist for every major family road trip. He certainly doesn't have to — especially because his kids are teens, and lord knows they could be plugged in and tuned out — but the whole family loves it. The playlist helps to keep them bonded as a family unit and opens the kids up to music they may not voluntarily choose on their own. He shares what he enjoys doing with those he loves. I've heard a few of these road-trip playlists, and they're pretty damn good. Sharing your gifts doesn't have to be huge or for a profit. Simply share your passion and what lights you up. Your vibration rises, and you'll raise the vibrations of others just by doing what you love. Nothing better than that.

A family friend makes a mean chocolate chip cookie. Every winter, when a group of twenty or so couples travels to Mexico, she bakes a bunch and brings them to the airport to share with her friends as they wait to board the plane. It's a simple gesture that brings both the giver and receiver pleasure. Try it! Start with something simple, and give it away—to a neighbor, a friend, or a perfect stranger. You can't tell me you don't get a boost, a natural high just from that one simple gesture. Imagine what the world would be like if we all did that on a regular basis. Pure magic!

In 2016, I was part of a production company that put on an event televised to the world with over fifty thousand people watching in person. It was, by far, the hardest, most stressful thing I have ever done. Like stressful to the point of wanting to vomit the minute I woke up in the morning knowing—or not knowing, for that matter—what the day would bring. My boss, an experienced producer in the live-events world, expected perfection from his staff. He was hard on us but only because he knew he hired the "A-Team." We were good at our jobs and could handle the pressure.

Throughout this process, I was pushed and challenged beyond any of my expectations, and because of this I learned so much about myself. I learned one of my gifts is being the lighthouse in the storm. I am good at staying calm in crisis, calming others, and moving forward with a level head. The biggest gift I learned about myself is that I'm an amazing multitasker and can create order from disorder. Without this experience, this event, I may not have ever recognized these strengths of mine, and now I move forward passionate in sharing my gifts with others.

Lesson one: Defining your gifts will help you find a passion.

an infinite love

PASSIONATE ABOUT PASSION

At one point I had gotten a little downtrodden with myself because, when the topic of passions came up in a conversation with a couple friends, I questioned myself and thought, *Man, I don't have any passions. There isn't one thing that's "my thing."* As I mentioned this, both friends responded and agreed, "Lisa, you're passionate about everything. Maybe you don't need just one thing." I liked that answer. They were right. I'm passionate for whatever I'm doing at that moment, and it seems to fluctuate on the regular. What always seems to ring true is that I'm passionate about helping others succeed with their passions. Supporting them in any way I can feels right and lights me up.

My dad was a professional athlete. He was good at just about every sport known to man, but that was never his true passion. Give him a nice summer day on a lake in a boat, a cold beer in one hand and a fishing pole in the other, and he will tell you, "This is exactly what heaven is." It makes me smile just thinking about it, not because I find any enjoyment in fishing but because that is his passion and he loves it. It fills his bucket and gives him life so that he can then share that joy and positive energy with his family.

A friend of mine is a high school hockey coach and a passionate one at that. Watching him in his element brings me so much dang happiness. His love for the game, the kids, and competition radiate with every arm gesture, pat on the back, and look on his face. When you find joy in something, it is easy to pass on that feeling of joy to others. People can pick up on your energy before you even utter a word.

lisa beck

Have you ever had one of those days where you're just not yourself? Maybe you're tired, stressed, or even feel something coming on. You haven't even made human contact with anyone yet that day, and as soon as you walk by someone, they say, "Oh, honey, what's wrong? You don't look so good." People can pick up on the energy you give off, so if your bucket is filled with joy, passion, excitement, and contentment from spending time doing something you love, people will see and feel that. You will impact their day in a positive way because you are being impacted in a positive way. And vice versa: if you never find a passion or never fill your bucket with anything that makes you happy—I repeat, makes *you* happy—people will pick up on that. And who wants to be around a Negative Nelly all day?

Lesson two: Find your passion and find joy in other people's passion. It will impact your life in a positive way.

LPGA, HERE I COME. JUST KIDDING . . . KINDA.

My most recent passion is golf. I love helping people break down their swing biomechanically and build a mobility and flexibility routine to help improve their game. I am also finding I love to play the sport myself. This came as quite a shock to me, as I have a lot of friends who are really good but I had never gotten into it. I realized this was due to some negative associations from my past.

When I was young, every Sunday was family day. In my recollection (and I'll have to check with my mom on this because she could remember it quite differently), we seemed to only do things my parents wanted to do, never anything my sister or I would have chosen. That meant

an infinite love

fishing and golf in the spring and summer, bird hunting in the fall, and skating or skiing in the winter. I enjoyed the skiing and skating, but the fishing, golfing, and bird hunting . . . not so much. My poor dad—we would go fishing, and here would be two young girls dragging their Barbie suitcases along. Our fishing boat would be filled with picnic supplies, tackle boxes, bait, a pee bucket, and Barbie accoutrements. So much Barbie gear!

When our family-day activity was golfing, my parents would take my sister and me along, and we would pray they only played nine holes because rarely would we rent a cart and only every once in a while did we get to swing a club. Talk about boredom for a young kid! Thus, my negative association with golf.

Fast-forward twenty-five years, and I knew I wanted to get into an activity that got me outside and moving. I couldn't decide between tennis and golf, and I just so happened to have a friend mention she was taking golf lessons. I thought, *Well, why not!* Four lessons later, I had new clubs, shoes, and outfits. Gotta have the outfits! I've also golfed more in the past month than I have in twenty-five years prior. I'm not good by any means, but I'm learning. I even joined a golf league. My recent passion for golf got me to step out of my comfort zone and do something a little scary for me. See, I don't like to not be good at something, especially in front of strangers. I was so afraid they would shun me or not want me to be in their golf foursome because I was new to the sport. I am learning to say screw that, release control, and dive in, and it feels so good.

Lesson three: Don't let negative associations or fear prevent you from finding new interests.

lisa beck

WHEN I GROW UP, I WANT TO BE A . . .

Another example of fear holding me back in my own life is building a business from the unknown. Over the years, I have dabbled in a lot of different jobs, from office manager of a restaurant to pizza delivery person, athletic trainer, personal trainer, leadership consultant, community relations expert, live event planner, and, at one point, even a researcher who got paid to look into local people who obtained DUIs. I've always felt I wanted to be a part of something bigger, and searching for what that looks like is a big part of my journey. I want to live my passion and not just "go to work." Never afraid of the hustle, I often dug in, and it worked until it didn't. Until I was burnt out and realized the passion was missing. Many times, after a little continuing-education course, I'd be right back in. But sometimes it was something else. I couldn't tell you what that something else was. All I knew was that I still felt unfulfilled.

About the time I started writing this book, I realized I needed to leave the health and fitness company I was working for and go off on my own. The company and owner were so great to me over the years, and I feel so fortunate to have a good relationship with the owner, but telling him I was leaving and that I had other aspirations was scary. He didn't want me to leave and kept offering me incentives to stay, including a partnership in his company. I accepted every incentive, yet I found nothing changed in the way I felt. It took starting the partnership proceedings for me to finally realize all of this was just a bandage on a cut that wasn't healing. I had to make a clean break and heal the cut on my own. I had signed a one-year noncompete, and walking away not knowing how I was going to make any money caused a lot of anxiety.

Of course, the negative self-talk set in, and I had to fight against the naysayers in my head. Add to this the fact that I knew I wanted to make more money, be a part of something bigger, follow my passions, and create a life of happiness but didn't know what the hell that looked like yet. How can you make money not even knowing what you want to do? I kept telling my friends, "I don't know what I want to be when I grow up." I didn't have a full vision for what I wanted to create. Sometimes I got overwhelmed with all the choices and ideas I had. I have a couple notebooks of business ideas that I never made a move on because at the time I thought I needed someone else to partner with to make it happen. The thought of doing it on my own was scary and overwhelming. It was like going to a restaurant and finding that the menu is as thick as a book; I couldn't decide what to order. In these situations, I usually end up panic-ordering and, more often than not, disappointed with my choice.

After I left the health and fitness company and started my own wellness company, I was determined to be happy, to choose happiness. I was determined to curate a life filled with happiness, where work didn't feel like work, passion was mixed with play, relationships mattered, and heart, authenticity, and kindness were my guide.

Lesson four: Taking a leap of faith and following a passion can lead to a more love-filled life—a love of who you are and what you do.

lisa beck

THE CANADIAN WILDERNESS IS CALLING YOU TO COME AND PLAY

As soon as I made this conscious choice to choose happiness and follow passion, things started to change. People, places, events, and appointments that were not in alignment with me anymore naturally started to fall away, and I noticed that as soon as I let go, serendipitous opportunities fell into my lap. One of these opportunities was the leadership retreat in Kenora, Canada, that I've mentioned previously. I was surrounded by top executives and senior leaders from around the world. We cried together, laughed together, shared meals, shared advice, and grew to be stronger, more powerful leaders in our personal and professional lives.

Our main activity throughout the week was to create our personal vision and mission statement. Again, right as I was questioning how I was going to curate my life of happiness, what I wanted to do, and where I wanted to go with my company, this exercise fell into my lap. I was forced to put thoughts and words to paper.

A year into creating my own life, I can say with absolute certainty that I am the happiest I have ever been (yeah!), making the least amount of money I have ever been (eek!), and at the moment still figuring out and exploring what my ultimate path looks like (go me!). I recognize that it may be having a hand in many things, but I know as long as I follow my mission statements, I am being true to myself.

My biggest lesson with this is that even though I'm not currently where I want to be financially, I know that, because I am following my passion and overcoming fears,

an infinite love

money and opportunities will follow if I put in the work. I understand I must stick to my boundaries and communicate with those around me when in pursuit of my passions. I also need to recognize who or what in my life may try to hold me back and how I can combat this.

I share with you my life's mission statement with the hope that you take a look at your own life and ask yourself, *What does it mean to follow my passion? What gifts do I have to offer the world? What does it look like for me to curate a life of contentment and pure happiness?* Whatever the answer may be, here's one thing I know is true: you will have to step out of your comfort zone and overcome your fears.

MY LIFE TRUTHS OR MISSION STATEMENTS
1. I am an empowering force of guiding light living my life from the heart.
2. Leading with bravery, I share the ups and downs of my journey in order to instill in others the feelings of freedom, love, and growth.
3. I create intimate connections based on respect and authenticity by challenging vulnerability in myself and showing kindness through my thoughts, words, and actions with all people who are important in my life.
4. I am a nurturing warrior embodying balance physically, mentally, and emotionally; living a life full of gratitude and vitality; and inspiring others to be ignited.

I still get chills every time I read my statements. Sometimes I think, *I wrote that? Huh, that's really good. Where the hell did I come up with those?* Truth is, I got vulnerable. I dug deep and listened to what my soul had to say. Now I know that, no matter what I do in life moving forward, I want to live and embody these four truths.

Lesson five: Be bold in the pursuit of your passions. Passion is about following the voices of your soul.

CALL TO ACTION

Write a list of activities, things, places, events, and causes that light you up.
- Why do you enjoy these things?
- How often are you participating in these events?
- What can you do to make more time for these passions?

Try a new activity or class.

Write down your gifts and ways you can share them with the world.

Share one of your gifts with someone.

Write down any fears that may be holding you back from trying new things or pursuing a life of happiness.
- What is your soul saying to you?
- What does a life filled with passion and happiness look like?

Take the time to watch those closest to you pursuing their passion or giving their gifts.
- How does this make you feel?
- How can you make time to do more of this?

CHAPTER NINE

Love the Grass in Your Own Backyard

"Every minute you spend wishing you had someone else's life is a minute spent wasting yours."
—Anonymous

For a few months, I was helping out my soul sister, Libby, by working at the front desk of her acupuncture business. One day, I was in a strange mood and came floating through the door announcing, "Guys, I was in some sort of mood when I got dressed today, but I'm feeling it so I'm going with it!" Just like the three-year-old picking out their outfit and wearing all the jewelry with a princess dress, Superman cape, neon colors, and mismatched socks, I was proud of my creation and rocking it. That particular day, I chose to wear black leggings with a black tank. Over that, I wore a long, sheer, multicolored swimsuit cover-up and black socks with coffee cups on them. All topped off by a high pony and red high tops. Every time Libby came to the front desk, she would look at me, laugh, and comment how she never has any doubt that I am always true to myself.

Wouldn't it be great if we could all say we are always true to ourselves? Unfortunately, that's not always the case, even in my world. Think about how much time we spend worrying about what others think and comparing ourselves to them. The data on my phone says I spent an average of thirty-five minutes on Instagram each day over the course of the past week. That's one form of social media—not included is time spent on Facebook, Twitter, Pinterest, Snapchat, YouTube, and the internet in general. This was a particularly busy week for me, so imagine what a slow week looks like. According to an article I read, the average person spends nearly two hours on social media each day. How many minutes are spent comparing one's life to another's? How many minutes are in judgment? How many of these minutes created positive emotions, and how many of these minutes caused feelings of being less than? We need to remember the grass is always greener in our own backyard.

FALLING DOWN THE RABBIT HOLE

I got sucked into an Instagram rabbit hole last night. You know, the kind where you blink and an hour has gone by, and you realize you've been looking at photos of people you don't even know. One page leads to another then to another and another. Before you realize it, you've gotten so far in that you don't even remember what you were originally looking at.

If we're not careful, that rabbit hole can be a slippery downward spiral of negative thoughts and I'm-notenoughs. A destructive self-worth hurricane swooping in unexpectedly and leaving a yard sale in its wake.

Many, many posts are viewed through rose-colored glasses. You know the post I'm talking about. The picture of a woman's perfect Pinterest living room. Not a book or plant out of place. No TVs hanging on the wall. How the hell does she do that with three kids, a dog, and a husband? How are there no toys strewn about? How are that plant and those breakables on the coffee table still standing? Do they even live there? Seriously, I live alone and it's a daily struggle to keep my house clutter-free.

People love to post pictures of themselves working out in which they are sporting minimal clothing and either barely look sweaty or somehow their sweat looks extremely sexy. I've seen the way I look after a workout. There is absolutely nothing sexy about the mascara raccoon eyes, frizzy dripping hair, and full-body imprint I leave on the floor from so much sweat.

I know these photos are photoshopped or taken by people who take so many pictures of themselves that they know all the tricks, yet there are days when I find myself comparing my body, my house, my fashion, and my life to those I see who seem picture-perfect on the 'Gram. Stop it! Stop it right now! Don't get sucked into a negative self-worth black hole. Recognize when you are heading down that road, and make a sharp left!

Recognize that you may not know the whole story. What is it that you are comparing, and how is it affecting your self-worth? What do you need to do so it doesn't affect you in a negative way? Maybe it's unfollowing, unliking, unfriending, not participating, or maybe even divorcing that particular person place or thing. You have a choice! You are the only one in control of you. Your decisions matter!

Lesson one: Honor and admire what you see in others, and then hard stop! Don't compare your life to theirs.

#FINSTAGRAM

Another thing that baffles my mind, and those of you with tweens or teens will know what I'm talking about, is the finstagram. I was catching up with my favorite teenage cousins and saw a notification pop up on my phone that one of them just added me as a friend on Instagram. I was so confused because I could have sworn we were already friends. Since we were all together, I had to ask. Our conversation was as follows:

Me: "Um, why did I just receive a notification that you are now following me on Instagram? Did you unfollow me? Am I not cool anymore? I always thought I was the cool cousin, guess I'm too old now." Insert sad face and eye roll. "And why is your name different?"

Teenager: "No, I still follow you with my Instagram account, now I also follow you with my finstagram account!"

Me: "Wait, back the truck up... What is a finstagram?"

Teenager: "It's my fake Instagram."

Me, royally confused: "Well, why do you need a fake Instagram?"

Teenager: "Because Instagram is where you post your artsy pretend life and finstagram is where you post about your real life and you are more selective on who you allow to follow you."

To me this made no sense and actually made me quite

sad. "Why can't you just post about your real life on your real account? Why do you need to pretend at all?"

She just laughed in response.

Lesson two: Honor your own self-worth. Stop caring about what others think. Be true to you. Be authentic.

SOCIAL MEDIA AND THE POSITIVITY FACTOR

I have always been and always will be a positive person. I always lean toward the good. If my sports team is down, I believe they are going to come through with the win. If I fall down, I know I'm getting back up. If I have a bad day, tomorrow will be better. Bad stuff happens, but I make a lot of effort to look for the positive. As much as I've talked about the negative effects social media can have on self-love, it can also be quite positive.

I love how you can connect with strangers around the world and start genuine friendships based on common interests and passions. I love how you can explore a whole new city just by exploring an Instagram page. One year, a friend and I went to Iceland for New Year's Eve (epic!) and I found the most awesome NYE pub crawl just by seeing an Instagram post on the city of Reykjavík. I attended a life-changing retreat in Costa Rica all because a friend liked an Instagram post. I love how you can get ideas, see what other people are reading, see the good other people are doing, see the struggles others feel like sharing, support reputable causes, and keep tabs on your family and friends.

My friend Megan, who lives in Ohio, started a nonprofit with other moms and their daughters in the neighborhood promoting positivity and spreading kindness.

an infinite love

She sent me some sweet swag and asked if I would wear the gear and promote the organization on social media. I couldn't wait to support such a wonderful cause and found I couldn't just wear the gear and not do something kind for someone, so I did just that. I received so much joy from performing a random act of kindness that I made a promise to myself that anytime I wore my new swag I had to do something kind for someone else.

Social media can make us feel connected. It can increase our self-love through sharing stories, spreading joy, and helping us to realize we are not alone. We do not have to travel this path by ourselves. There is someone else out there who can be our cheerleader, hold our hand, listen to us cry, cheer us on, swap stories, and hold a space for understanding. That is powerful, that is positive, and that is what we need more of.

Lesson three: Make the choice to practice and promote positive self-worth through social media.

THE CHERRY ON TOP

The grass is always greener in your own backyard. No one spends all their time, money, water, and attention watering the neighbor's lawn. You spend it on your own yard, your own property. No one wants to pay the water bill watering the lawns of the entire neighborhood. Spend the time and energy taking care of your own yard, and be proud of the grass you grew—brown patchy parts and all! Instagram that, and hashtag it #MyGrassIsGreenToo, my friends.

CALL TO ACTION

Do a digital detox.
- What or whom do you need to delete from your social media platform?
- Make an effort to spend less time on social media and more time in the present.

Follow social media accounts that spread positivity or give you daily affirmations.

Reflect on a time in recent months when you compared yourself or your life to others.

Make a list of some things you can do to increase your own self-worth.
- Make an effort to try one thing each day.

Answer the question: What does it mean to water your own backyard?

CHAPTER TEN

Lost and Not Found: Balance

"Balance is not something you find, it's something you create."

—Jana Kingsford

When we aren't taking care of ourselves, physically, mentally, emotionally, and spiritually, we can't take care of others physically, mentally, emotionally, and spiritually. Finding balance in our lives is a crucial step to showing ourselves more love. It is not lost on me that I write this chapter during the Libra season, around the fall equinox. An equal balance of day and night, light and dark in the sky. Balance is the theme of the season and zodiac.

MASCULINE VS. FEMININE ENERGY

In the spiritual world, there is a concept called Divine Masculine and Divine Feminine. In layman's terms, we are talking about masculine energy and feminine energy. It's not a male or female thing. Every person needs a balance of both to be in harmony. Masculine energy is strong, protective, supportive, proactive, courageous, systematic, powerful, confident, energized, passionate, and able to surrender to the feminine. All great traits, but if out of balance, masculine energy can be ruthless, destructive, aggressive, selfish, egoistic, threatened, disconnected, arrogant, headstrong, forceful, and cruel.

A balanced feminine energy is compassionate, wise, creative, fluid, nurturing, whole, passionate, intuitive, abundant, egoless, sexual, truth-seeking, self-caring, able to express emotions, and assertive. The opposite, out-of-balance feminine energy is depressed, needy, codependent, overly sensitive, self-pitying, self-doubting, victimized, gossiping, selfish, jealous, manipulative, self-comparing, people-pleasing, and controlling.

Let's be honest, we've all at some point been a healthy dose of both the positive and negative sides of both energies. How do we stay balanced between masculine and feminine and stay in the positive attributes of each?

It starts with recognition. Take a look at your own life and ask yourself where you fit in. Which of these traits, the positive and negative, do you find in yourself? Where do the positive traits show up? When are you flowing in your Divine Feminine and Divine Masculine? When do you notice the negative traits show up? What situations are you in? What roles are you playing? Are you out of balance with these energies at work, at home, with friends and family, or in clubs or organizations?

I work in a male-dominated industry. I always have. My first job was at a golf course. From athletic training, to live-event planning, to health and fitness, it's amazing to

an infinite love

see the number of women double and triple in these fields over the years, but they are still predominantly male. I see myself as a natural teacher and a natural leader, and with these gifts come a lot of masculine traits. Although they are positive ones, they are at many times out of balance with my feminine energy.

I make a point to include more feminine energy into my life. I do this physically by getting my hair done and getting pampered. When meeting friends for dinner, I make a point of enjoying the ritual of dressing myself up: hair, makeup, accessories, clothes. I also honor my feminine by slowing down and enjoying the world around me. I get out in nature. And I make sure I do something creative, such as writing, reading, cooking, making up games with my niece and nephew, dancing to music, or making my space homey.

In myself, I recognized that being a nurturer, which can be a positive feminine trait if in balance, can become a negative trait when I continually put other people's needs above my own. I was continually putting others' needs ahead of mine, and my self-care was at the bottom of my to-do list. I couldn't even recognize how out of balance I was.

I am fiercely independent, and as great of a trait as that can be, it can also be detrimental. My ability to ask for help was nonexistent. I didn't want to look weak and incapable, which are out-of-balance masculine traits, so I took it all on and on and on. This is when burnout happens. Burnout from career, family, and life.

Being able to ask for help is a positive feminine and masculine trait, as it opens you up to receive, to be in flow (feminine) and attract abundance (feminine and masculine).

This give-and-take of masculine and feminine energy is never more present than when I watch my dog Daks play with his bestie Sadie. My male dog is full of energy and always eager, ready, and willing to get his play on. Sadie, the ever-wise woman, will engage with him until she's had enough and then, cool and collected, walk away. Setting up boundaries! Daks, being a typical male, will bound up to her—wink wink, nudge nudge, poke poke, let's get our play on. Sadie will give him the good ole side eye and walk away unimpressed.

This is the point when you see their roles switch. Accepting that he came forward with too much masculine energy, Daks will lie on his back, opening himself up to her, being patient, silent, and vulnerable and waiting for her to initiate play. After recognizing this, I've watched Sadie walk over and take on the masculine role. She will be playful and aggressive in the most gentle way. They will go back and forth like this, reverting between masculine and feminine energy all night long. Completely in balance with each other and completely in sync with their own energy.

Lesson one: To be in harmony with yourself, find a balance of masculine and feminine energies. Self-care is recognizing when you are out of balance and which energy you need to honor more.

THE PERMISSION SERIES
Work-life balance is a trendy idea. I'm all for companies allowing more flexibility and creativity in how they view

an infinite love

the standard work environment. Studies have shown this can increase productivity, boost morale, and create a positive work culture. However, our professional environment is only one aspect of our lives where we have a need for balance. I think we have done a great job at ignoring what balance means in our personal lives. One aspect of a healthy life balance is what I call the Permission Series: Permission to let go. Permission to be selfish with your time and energy. Permission to not care. Permission to not have the answer.

Permission to Let Go
So often, we set unrealistic goals and lack boundaries for ourselves. We aim to be the best friend, coworker, parent, and human possible. This is not balanced energy. Why do we do this to ourselves? Why do we push, push, push beyond what we are physically or mentally capable of handling?

Now, I *am* a firm believer in pushing and challenging yourself and making yourself step out of your comfort zone to grow, learn, and change, but the aforementioned type of pushing is different. That type of push is pushing to please others and is an energy suck. Pushing and challenging yourself should be scary but invigorating at the same time.

Everyone's goal should be to live a balanced life. A balance of push and pull physically, mentally, spiritually, and emotionally. This starts with an understanding of when it's time to let yourself off the hook. Sometimes balance looks like slowing way down and letting go. When you let something go, you also make room for something new to enter. This something new is often bigger, better, and brighter. Letting go can be freeing.

Permission to Be Selfish with Your Time and Energy
The other day, my sister called me. Barely above a whisper, she said, "Hey, how's it going?"

"Why are we whispering?" I asked.

"I'm hiding in my closet, hoping my kids won't find me. I need a five-minute break or I'm going to lose it on them!"

I had to laugh. Love doesn't even begin to describe what I feel toward my niece and nephew, but I understand where my sister is coming from. She is a phenomenal mom with more patience than anyone I've ever met, but even she needs a break. She is a great example of giving herself permission. Permission to be selfish with her time and energy. In this case, permission to run away from her kids and hide in the closet with a glass of wine and some adult conversation.

Whether you are a new mom or a parenting veteran, it is OK to take time for yourself away from your kids. Even if it is five minutes folding laundry while listening to your self-love playlist or running to the grocery store without the kids. It is important to be open in communicating your needs to your significant other, and they should be willing to take on parenting duty so you can step away.

Permission to Not Care
Give yourself permission to not care what other people think or how they react to your decisions. Only you know what is best for you.

an infinite love

My friends had me over for dinner one warm summer evening. When your friend's husband is a chef, you always accept dinner invitations. His paella was everything my taste buds could dream of. At the time both of their kids were quite young, so getting them to sit still for more than five minutes at the dinner table was a battle of epic proportions. A fluid adult conversation was not happening.

I remember they both felt so bad and kept apologizing for their kids. The only thing that kept the kids quiet and sitting for a solid fifteen minutes was when they turned to bribery and gummy bears. "Don't judge our parenting skills," they said. "We just want some adult conversation." They were so concerned about what I thought. I laughed and said, "Don't even bat an eye about it. I get it!" If this sounds like your household around dinnertime, give yourself permission. You can't always win the gold star for parenting, and that's OK. Fill your house with love, and the rest will work itself out.

I'm going to repeat this because I feel it is too important to only say once: Give yourself permission to not care what other people think or how they react to your decisions. Only you know what is best for you and yours.

This was and still is a particularly hard lesson for me to learn. It's easy to say, "IDGAF what anyone thinks about me," but let's get real: that's not the truth. I will admit, I like to be liked. Who doesn't? I care what other people think of me. I care about how I'm perceived, especially by my close friends and family. I want their support in my decisions, and many times I have it, but sometimes I don't.

I've aimed to focus more on not caring what strangers and others with whom I don't have a vested relationship think of me, not catering myself just to be liked by someone else, and not basing my choices on what other people think. The more you get to really know and fall in love with yourself, the better you understand and accept who you truly are and what you need. What you need most definitely will look, sound, and feel different than what anyone else on this earth needs. What makes us so amazing is the fact that we are all such awesome, unique people.

Permission to Not Know the Answer
April showers bring May flowers, or so the saying goes. In Minnesota, April brings thundersnow. If you've never experienced thundersnow, let me tell you, it's a confusing, WTF-is-happening experience. It's when the weather doesn't know what the hell it's doing and so ultimately does everything all at once. Thunder, lightning, snow, possibly some form of rain, and sun all appear at the same time. Sometimes the Universe can't make up her mind either. I get you, girl, I get you!

I reference this meteorological phenomenon to bring light to the fact that sometimes we just don't know WTF we are doing, and that is 100-percent OK. We come across a situation and we throw every resource into solving the problem. Sometimes this works, but most often it's a quick fix until we slow down and figure out what's underneath. In the case of the thundersnow, with time, the weather calms down, the sun warms the earth, and April showers do eventually bring May flowers.

Lesson two: Add more balance to your life by giving

an infinite love

yourself permission to let go, to be selfish with your time and energy, to not care what other people think, and to not know the answer. Balance will help dissolve stress and ignite a sense of freedom in your life.

PUT YOURSELF FIRST
Balance is making the time to attend to your own needs. My sister recognized she didn't do a great job putting herself first after having child numero uno, so she made sure to do exactly that after numero dos. She was going to do what worked best for her. I repeat: *what worked best for her*. Everyone is different and must find the balance that works best for them in each situation. Putting yourself first can have many different meanings and actions.

For my sister, this included not feeling guilty when she decided she was going to stop breastfeeding when she went back to work, finding more time for her girlfriends, leaning on her husband more, and booking a girls' weekend getaway.

In my life, putting myself first meant creating a list of nonnegotiables: things I choose to do every day in order to fulfill myself. They are an integral part of my self-care and happiness and include making my bed, walking my dog, moving my body, meditating, and writing in my gratitude journal. This means no matter what is going on, no matter how busy my schedule is, I make a commitment to myself and rarely skip these items.

It's never too late to start putting yourself first. That is a big step in adding more balance to your life. Put yourself first to take care of you. Do what needs to be done so you can be the best version of yourself. No one wants to be around an empty tank of a person. It serves no one to let your tank run low.

Lesson three: Finding balance is making an effort to serve yourself so you can serve others in turn.

GUILT BE GONE

We've talked about finding physical balance, whether it be playing more and working less, scheduling time for yourself, or saying no to social obligations, but finding mental balance can be a tougher trek. Mental balance has a huge impact on our overall happiness and self-love. For example, guilt can be our biggest frenemy.

As a good friend usually does, guilt can drive us to learn, grow, and improve. Let's say you gave someone your word but for whatever reason didn't follow through. You may feel guilty because you let them down. You didn't intentionally try to hurt or disappoint, but the truth is you did. Guilt can cause us to look internally and ask the harder questions. *What stopped me from following through?* Maybe the answer was you were too busy, afraid of failure or judgment, or lacked self-worth. There could be a whole host of reasons. *Why did I say yes in the first place? A wanting of love, of acceptance, of self-satisfaction, a feeling of I-can-do-it-all?* By taking this guilty feeling and doing a little deeper digging, we can then ask, *OK, next time how do I honor my true self?* You can channel this guilt into action and improvement.

Guilt can be your enemy when you take the same scenario and overcompensate in all areas. One guilty thought in one situation turns to a hundred guilty thoughts for multiple situations. Or you try to overcompensate, think-

an infinite love

ing, *I let you down once, so I'm going to do all the things to prove to you* (or rather to myself) *that I'm worthy* (of your love, forgiveness, affection, praise, friendship, etc.). In chapter 2, we talked about divorcing negative thoughts, words, and actions. Finding mental balance is recognizing when these seep in, seeing them for what they are, and then taking inspired action instead of overcompensating.

An example of this would be as follows: Let's say we have two people. Both work for the same company, and their positions are going to be terminated. Both parties need to find a new job.

Person One is feeling guilty because they've known about the termination for the past three months but haven't really done much of a job search. They decide this weekend they are going all-in and really hitting the pavement. They are applying to all the jobs, running around town handing out resume after resume, and hoping someone bites. Person One doesn't even care if the job doesn't meet any of their wants and needs; they just want the security of a new position. This, my friends, is overcompensation.

Person Two knows they are busy at work and that's going to make the job search really hard, but they have faith and trust that the right opportunity will present itself. On their lunch break, they decide to run to the dry cleaner to drop off a bag of clothes that has been sitting in their closet for the past month. Randomly, they run into a former coworker at the dry cleaner. Catching up, Person Two mentions their current position is going to be terminated. The former coworker then remembers his neighbor was just talking about his new startup and brought up that he was looking for someone with Person Two's exact talents. In fact, the former coworker was going to see the neighbor that evening at poker night and would pass along contact information. Inspired action is not panicking, but rather listening to the inner inklings of your soul. I can without a doubt tell you that the best opportunities I've ever come across have been from a place of inspired action. I've been inspired to do or say something, and there has been a snowball effect of connections.

Lesson four: Mental balance is ridding yourself of guilt and taking inspired action instead.

KRYPTONITE IS *NOT* BALANCE

Now, when I say give yourself permission, it does come with a caveat. Don't go overboard if you have a kryptonite. Balance is *not* an excuse!

Let's say you are trying to lose some weight, but it's national donut day and you choose to partake and consume this wonderful maple bacon soft deliciousness of a donut. Enjoy, be happy, and then proceed on. Honor it for what it is and how it makes you feel in that moment. Don't let this donut lead to french fries at lunch and pizza at dinner and then all of a sudden it's been two or three days in a row of donut deliciousness.

Or let's say you decide to be selfish with your time and energy, so you say no to a social function. You find you really enjoyed your time to yourself, so all of a sudden you are saying no to all social functions all the time because your couch and Netflix are just too simple.

It's best to name your kryptonite — something you enjoy but that, if you allow yourself to enjoy it too much,

an infinite love

will swing you off balance and into detrimental territory. Maybe you start out with the best intentions in the name of self-care, but if not careful this can lead to bad decisions or self-destruction.

Lesson five: Recognizing the kryptonite in your life will allow you to maintain a healthy physical, mental, and emotional balance.

CALL TO ACTION

Make a list of your masculine and feminine energies.
- Are you in balance?
- Is there one energy you need to honor more?
- Write down some steps you can take to accomplish a balance.

Write down areas of your life in which you need to give yourself more permission.
- Are you too hard on yourself in certain situations or areas?
- Create a mantra you can say or write to help get you in the mindset of permission.

Write down ways you can put yourself first in your day, week, and month.
- What are your nonnegotiables that need to happen in order to serve yourself?

Banish your guilt! Make a list of times in the past that you experienced some guilt.
- List ways you can take inspired action instead of overcompensation.

Name your kryptonite.
- Create a list of all the people, places, things, or situations that could lead to self-destruction.
- How can you avoid them or create safe boundaries?

CHAPTER ELEVEN

Oh My God She's Naked

"Being vulnerable is the only way to allow your heart to feel true pleasure."

— Bob Marley

I believe nature is a great teacher. Many life lessons can be learned by paying attention to the world around us. As I was walking my pup on a lovely fall day, I noticed a particular leaf lying on the ground, so I picked it up. There were a bunch of flashy leaves of various color combinations to choose from, but the one I picked, or what was left of it, was plain brown. The leaf obviously was quite the tasty lunch for some creature, yet it was one of the most beautiful leaves I'd ever seen. I couldn't help but notice and admire it. Upon closer examination, it felt so fragile in my hands. And it was, yet it wasn't. All its "fluff" and leafy parts had been eaten away and the only thing left was its skeleton, but this leaf was in perfect condition. Its entire framework was still intact. The leaf was baring its soul.

Everything was taken away but what it was at its core. It was fragile and so vulnerable yet surviving and strong. It was beautiful and perfectly imperfect. Being vulnerable can be perfectly imperfect.

THE POWER OF VULNERABILITY

I'm a believer in signs—signs from the Universe, signs that smack you in the face loud and clear. One day before I sat down to write, I meditated and asked for guidance to help the words flow. A new chapter on vulnerability popped into my head. I jotted the idea down and started to write, feeling distracted and unsure where I was going with this subject. I moved on with my day and thought, *OK, sidebar that topic for a while. I promise I'll come back to it.*

But it turns out the Universe wouldn't let me procrastinate for long. Twenty minutes later, I was flipping through some old notes on my phone and saw that at some point in recent months I wrote down "The Power of Vulnerability by Brené Brown." Huh! I wasn't even sure what this was: a book, documentary, podcast? In fact, I don't even think I'd ever heard of Brené Brown at that point. Obviously, whenever, wherever I heard "power of vulnerability," it must have struck a chord with me. Then, like most things in my life, I got busy and forgot all about it. But this day—the day I meditated and asked for guidance, the day I had the idea to include a chapter on vulnerability—I came across that note.

Fast-forward to two hours later. I was eating lunch with a friend, and I mentioned to him lately I'd been getting into some leadership coaching. I asked if he had any recommendations for good podcasts or books in the

an infinite love

self-improvement genre. I'll give you one guess as to what he suggested—yup, *The Power of Vulnerability* by Brené Brown. I just started laughing. (Inspired action at its finest!)

This subject of vulnerability may be one of the biggest life lessons for me to learn and consequently unlearn old habits. OK, Universe, I'm here. I fully understand that I need to take a lesson in vulnerability by writing about it. Here I go . . .

Be vulnerable . . . Ugh! Just typing that conjures up a big lump in my throat! A pit in my stomach and a sort of sickness. Why do I feel this way? Because being vulnerable is scary as shit! People see the real you. Your mask is removed. When I'm vulnerable, I'm no longer the strong, powerful female warrior I am just learning to become. *Excuse me, but your soul is showing!* How embarrassing! How scary! I mean, I've been the girl that's come out of the bathroom and had toilet paper stuck to her shoe, leaving a trail down the middle of the airplane. (Obviously, my seat was the farthest from the bathroom.) Or worse, at an awards banquet honoring my dad, my dress somehow got tucked into my undies, exposing waaay more than I ever intended. But not even those incidences trump being truly vulnerable. That's probably why it's taken me more than a year to write this book. I can claim writer's block, but deep down I know that I don't want to sit down to write because I'm writing from my heart and exposing my soul. I'm putting my thoughts, emotions, and lessons on paper and opening myself up. I'm being vulnerable.

The funny thing is, I have no problem being vulnerable on stage, dancing, speaking, and singing (even though

I'm an awful singer). But with these activities, the way I view it, it's not about me; it's about the audience and about entertainment.

I'm a great listener, and when I listen, I want people to be their true, most authentic selves with me. Somehow I can always get the other person to crack open and be vulnerable with me, but when it comes to me returning the favor, I often think, *Oh, I don't want to burden them with my issues. My life isn't that interesting. I don't have much to speak about*, and so on and so forth. But ask any of my friends and they'll tell you I lead a fascinating life because I'm always on some new adventure, whether it be a trip, job, project, or idea. They're like, "Lis, I've done nothing but laundry, sit on the toilet for hours with my kid waiting for him to poop, and fall asleep ten minutes into the Netflix show my husband and I were supposed to watch together. You've been to more new restaurants in a month than I've been to in two years."

Yet my response when people ask what or how I'm doing is usually an "I'm all good! Nothing new or exciting here," or some other generic answer that doesn't really tell them anything.

Often, I'm really happy and everything is all good, but I still struggle to open up and talk about my feelings, successes, failures, lessons, or what new adventure I have taken on. I keep telling myself stories so that I don't have to be vulnerable in front of anyone.

This has been a huge learning process for me, and as scary as it is, I'm starting to make some progress. I've recognized that my unwillingness to share my triumphs and sticky-icky tribulations is based solely on caring too

an infinite love

much about how other people viewed me. I don't want to seem braggy about my accomplishments or to make them feel less than, and I don't want to discuss my hardships to make myself seem less than. Kind of a lose-lose situation, if you think about it! I can't control how others feel, and yes, I should be sensitive to their feelings, but it should never stop me from being proud of myself and talking about it. The people you surround yourself with should be by your side celebrating your accomplishments and also have an open ear to listen and guide you when things are tough. After all, being open and truly vulnerable makes a female warrior infinitely stronger and creates a better connection with her people.

Lesson one: Being vulnerable can seem scary, but ultimately it creates deeper connections with yourself and others.

CONFRONTING VULNERABILITY

Brené Brown's "The Power of Vulnerability" speech is one of the most-watched TED Talks ever. This shows what an important topic vulnerability is and that, even though we aren't talking enough about it, people are willing to listen. For most people, the word "vulnerable" conjures up feelings of fear and weakness, but Brown says that vulnerability is the exact opposite. It's the birthplace of joy, love, creativity, and belonging. In her book *Daring Greatly*, Brown writes, "Vulnerability is the core of all emotions and feelings. To foreclose on our emotional life out of a fear that the costs will be too high is to walk away from the very thing that gives purpose and meaning to life."

I don't know about you, but a more meaningful life

definitely sounds like something I want. Love, connection, courage, clarity, creativity, and passion all stem from a place of vulnerability. Yes to all of that please!

Brown says, "Our willingness to own and engage with our vulnerability determines the depth of our courage and the clarity of our purpose." She believes the level to which we protect ourselves from being vulnerable is a measure of our fear and disconnection. Those that have the hardest shell have the most fear. She says, "Perfect and bulletproof are seductive, but they don't exist in the human experience." Amen, sister. Amen.

Lesson two: Being vulnerable isn't scary or being weak. It's courageous and allows you to feel and be real.

CONTROL, YOU'RE NOT WELCOME HERE ANYMORE

A dear friend of mine hired me to help her find and create better balance with her thriving small business and busy home life. We found her personal bucket was completely drained, as she was giving all her energy to her growing business, volunteering, and the needs of her daughter. She had recently hired employees to help on the business side but was not taking advantage of all they could offer. These employees offered a chance to handle the busywork, take simple responsibilities off her plate, and help increase revenue. She had big plans for her new team but felt stuck, and nothing was moving forward.

What she couldn't see, and what I helped her recognize, was that she was afraid of relinquishing control. She had employees eagerly waiting to use their talents to help support her business, which in turn would let her focus on

an infinite love

other creative endeavors she wanted to pursue. Her block was her own love, passion, and hard work of building a small business from the ground up. This business was her baby, and putting any aspect in the hands of others scared her. However, if she mustered up the courage and opened herself up to being vulnerable by relinquishing control, time and space for creativity would increase and she would begin to fill her own bucket with abundant energy.

Any new parent dropping off their child at day care for the first time goes through the exact same lesson. You can do all the research and choose a large corporate center, immersion day care, small in-home day care, relatives, or an in-home nanny, but it doesn't matter; when you walk out that door, you are forced to be vulnerable and relinquish control to someone else having a hand in influencing and caring for your child. You may cry as hard as your child when you leave them, but as you do it day after day, you will cry a little less as you get used to this new normal. You will realize that your child is now getting a whole new perspective on love, nurturing, and connection.

Being vulnerable is the start to living and leading an authentic life. When you are leading an authentic life, you are fully loving yourself the most.

Lesson three: Vulnerability is the source of joy and creativity when you open yourself up and relinquish control.

TIME TO TAKE OFF THE MASK

In his book *The Mask of Masculinity*, Lewis Howes speaks about nine different types of masks men wear, hiding their vulnerability in different forms. Only through self-discovery and removing these masks can someone truly find love, be love, and live a joyous, authentic life. Even though his book is geared toward men, I found I could relate to a lot, and it also helped me as a female to understand how to communicate better with men and what they are trying to say without saying anything.

My college degree is in athletic training, so in the past I have worked with and been surrounded by many athletes of various skill levels, from little tykes just starting out, to the pervasive weekend warriors, to professionals. One of the masks Lewis Howes writes about is the "Athlete Mask." Howes—a former professional athlete and now an author, public speaker, and lifestyle entrepreneur—speaks a lot about how athletes' self-worth gets so tied up in their sport and performance that they lose their authenticity. Self-worth and vulnerability go hand in hand.

Athletes, especially those at the higher level, spend years of their lives following the same routine. They get up, eat, and head to practice, meetings, and maybe a team event or competition in the evening. Home or away, they establish a routine day in and day out. It becomes so consistent that they don't even think about it anymore. On game days, they may eat at the same restaurant, order the same meal, arrive at the venue at the same time, put equipment on in the same order, and so on. They know their role and their place in the pecking order. It's familiar, it's safe, it's comfortable.

But then these athletes get a major injury that takes them out for an extended period of the season, or maybe at the end of the year they choose or are forced to retire. Their whole world is shaken up and flipped upside down.

an infinite love

I've seen this many times: athletes whose careers are now over or are in question go into a bit of a depression. They don't know their role in life anymore. They don't know who they are if they aren't playing their sport. They don't have a purpose. If you ask any retired athlete what they miss the most, it typically isn't the competitions, wins, or losses; it's the bus rides, hotel rooms, dinners, and bonds with teammates. At the end of the day, being disconnected is a big fear of not only athletes but everyone.

As women, many of us learn how to deal with emotions from a young age. Women have a natural tendency to seek help and talk about their feelings. We have learned how to have a good cry, pick ourselves up, and move on with life knowing that it will probably happen again. We learn to rely on our support system and know it gets easier as we go along.

But society teaches men that in order to "be a man" you must be tough and not show emotions. In my experience with male athletes, and many men in general, who all of a sudden are told they don't measure up, don't know how to process the emotions that go along with rejection and disconnection. They don't know how to confront their vulnerability. They are seen as tough, strong, and resilient and always have been. They can't be seen as sullen or weak, cry, or be emotional—especially in front of their fans, coworkers, and family. Many hide away what they are truly feeling instead of taking off their masks, being vulnerable, and feeling all the feels. Have you ever been in a similar situation? When have you been afraid to confront your vulnerability?

I encourage you to take off the mask. Be yourself, love

yourself, and heal yourself. Change can be hard, but it can also be great. Confront vulnerability head on, embrace all emotions, and champion what is to come. Greatness awaits!

Lesson four: We must own our vulnerability and confront it head on. Take off the mask.

STOP NUMBING EMOTIONS

You can't selectively hide or numb your emotions. Life is a pendulum of emotions, and we must feel them all. Newton's third law goes like this: for every action, there is an equal and opposite reaction. If we numb fear, we numb love. If we numb sadness, we numb joy. If we numb failure, we numb success.

Why and how we numb is different for everyone, but we each have a way to justify our choice. All too often, we turn to vices—alcohol, drugs, food, sex, bingeing TV, keeping our world small, or perfectionism on the outside—to hide from our vulnerability.

It took me a while to recognize where I have a hard time being vulnerable in my own life. I know I crave connection. I wanted to build connections in my romantic relationships, but you can't have connection without vulnerability, and subconsciously I wasn't willing to reach the level of vulnerability that is required to create deep, intimate relationships with partners. I didn't have a need to. I always had roommates and a solid core group of friends who met all my emotional needs. Anyone I was dating got leftovers. Imagine trying to build a strong, solid relationship on emotional leftovers. It's not going to work. Often I wouldn't date because I recognized this, and it was easier

an infinite love

not to invest anything. No one got hurt this way. Life is about taking risks, growing, and leaning into challenges. I was doing the exact opposite.

It wasn't until all my friends started getting married and having families, while I was living alone and lacked an "emotional partner," that I realized I was hiding my emotions.

I had to figure out why I was having a hard time being vulnerable in relationships, and I recognized one part of it stemmed from the fear of losing my freedom. I didn't want to relinquish control of my own life and my own emotions. Funny thing is, a true partner would never take away your freedom and never try to control the person you are. They want to see you in your authenticity and love you because of it.

I discovered another part of my struggle with vulnerability was due to a generational tie. My dad's side of the family comes from German lineage. Culturally, German Americans come across as stubborn, strong, and stoic. Outwardly expressing emotions is not our norm. We learn this from our parents, who learned it from their parents, and so on up the chain.

All the more reason my mom is such a good partner for my father. She balances our family emotionally. She has always made it clear how important it is to talk about our emotions and that suppression only leads us down a dangerous path either hurting ourselves or others. My fifteen-year-old self hated talking things out—let me fester in my teenage angst!—but my adult self is quite grateful. I came to the understanding that I subconsciously picked up on my stoic German American family traits. Showing love and being a loving partner looked like keeping my emotions to myself. I believed showing emotion was a sign of weakness and neediness. I didn't want anyone to think I was needy. I was a strong, independent woman.

Recognizing where you have trouble showing vulnerability is the first step in fixing it because it gives you a choice: continue on the same path with the same results, or grow and change. Even today, after some solid self-work and recognition, my fears creep up now and then. Where in your life do you recognize you have a hard time showing vulnerability?

We've all heard the phrase, "Do one thing a day that scares you." I used to brush that saying off, but now I really try to embrace it. What scares you? Lean in. Chances are, if you are feeling vulnerable, so is someone else. Let's not make it harder than it is. Why are we hiding? Why are we so ashamed of ourselves? Why are we so afraid to let ourselves be seen—like, really seen? What is one small step you can take each day to make vulnerability less scary and more exciting? We all could benefit from practicing more vulnerability.

Lesson five: Embracing vulnerability is recognizing, feeling, and talking about your emotions.

COMMUNICATION IS KEY

As evident from the previous lessons in this chapter, many times we can't confront vulnerability without communication. Throughout our lives, we will need to have crucial conversations with partners, children, bosses, employees, parents, teammates, and friends. Any crucial conversation takes an act of courage. I bet we can all think of a time

an infinite love

a conversation didn't go as planned. Emotions took over, walls as strong as Fort Knox came up, defense tactics were in full force, and gunfire came from each side. Conversations such as these will send vulnerability packing.

In the book *Crucial Conversations: Tools for Talking When the Stakes Are High*, the authors discuss ways to have difficult conversations. I took away three key markers to keep in mind that will make the conversation, as hard as it may be, more successful for each participant.

Create Safety

When going into a crucial conversation, it's imperative you ask yourself ahead of time, *What is the goal of this convo? What am I looking to get out of this?* No one wants to feel attacked when being talked to, because then adrenaline takes over and everyone immediately gets defensive. Instead of communication, you get a fight-or-flight response. Finding a mutual purpose between parties creates safety. It's also important to remember that we communicate not only with our words but also with our body language. Look at your body language. Is your body or positioning creating a feeling of welcoming, openness, and safety, or are you closed off and trying to establish dominance?

Create Open Dialogue

You must care enough about the interests of others to hear what they are saying. Try to see the other person's side, and let them know it is safe to share their point of view. Even if you don't agree, letting the other person use their voice emphasizes safety and creates a more relaxed atmosphere where conversation can flow back and forth. This is where people will open up and feel more comfortable being vulnerable.

Be an Empathetic Listener
Be sincere. Don't just listen to what the other person is saying, but really pay attention and understand. Be curious. Instead of reacting in fear, ask yourself what is causing the other person to react this way. What stories are they telling themself? Be patient. When in conversation, slow down. Think before you speak, and take control of your emotions in the conversation. You can't listen when you are so focused on your own story and your own emotions.

Lesson six: When having an emotionally charged conversation with others, it's important to create safety, keep an open dialogue, and listen. This will allow vulnerability to shine.

LET'S WRAP UP THIS VULNERABILITY THING ALREADY

In *Daring Greatly*, Brown talks about walking into "the arena" with courage and the willingness to engage. We must love ourselves enough to walk into the arena, whether that arena is a hard conversation with your partner, public speaking, quitting your job, starting a new chapter in life, raising children, making an important call, or rising up without fear and trepidation. Recognize that vulnerability can be a bit complicated and takes a great amount of courage but leads to a more fulfilling, self-satisfied life. That is infinite love for yourself.

CALL TO ACTION

Write down what being vulnerable means to you.
- How can vulnerability improve your relationships?

Journal about times in your life you have a hard time being vulnerable.
- What emotions were you suppressing and why?

What type of mask do you find yourself wearing?
- Why do you think you wear this particular mask?
- Is there something from your childhood that caused you to put on the mask?

Make a point to practice vulnerability in one area of your life. Lead with your heart.

Watch Brené Brown's TED Talk, "The Power of Vulnerability."

Write about a time a crucial conversation you had went wrong.
- What could you have done to create safety and an open dialogue?

CHAPTER TWELVE

Be Your Own Hero

"No one can make you feel inferior without your consent."

—Eleanor Roosevelt

"Knock knock!"
"Who's there?"
"Self-worth."
"Self-worth who?"
"Exactly!"

TAKE YOUR POWER BACK

Dictionary.com defines self-worth as "a sense of one's own value as a human being."

That's powerful. Don't put that power in other's hands; keep that power to yourself! That's your superhuman strength.

During a conversation about dating and life with my ride-or-die, Carrie, she said, "Girl, you need to take your power back!" I had to sit back and think. *What does she*

an infinite love

mean? What power am I giving away, and what exactly do I have to take back?

As women doing, achieving, and being it all, what bargains do we make? What do we end up sacrificing at the cost of our own self-worth and happiness? How self-destructive are we by our own hand, by not following our calling, by settling, by not speaking our truth, by surrendering our power to others? We need to stop and step out of this box. We need to shatter this misconception that we as women have to be the martyrs and have to sacrifice our hopes and dreams for the sake of friends, family, children, work, or our own past choices.

As women, we are naturally passionate, creative, intuitive, and nurturing. But many times, these traits lay dormant and not fully amplified to our full potential. We aren't honoring our full self-worth.

We go about our lives and love, work, play, celebrate, cry, and do all the things, but do we really *live*? Do we live with vigor and joy? Do we challenge and push ourselves to pursue the dreams that lay deep within our soul? Do we take the time to listen to our own inner voice and what our soul is whispering to us?

Clarissa Pinkola Estés speaks to this in her book *Women Who Run with the Wolves*. She writes: "Her metamorphosis has no metabolism."

There is no fire in her belly. Her power, her growth, is stunted by her own fear and unknowing. Her own excuses shut out the whispers stirring inside.

We absolutely cannot be afraid of our own power, but as women, and men too, we are. We are afraid of the true greatness that lies inside each and every one of us. This is because we know it could bring us extreme joy, self-satisfaction, and even success, as defined in each person's eyes, but we also know the journey to joy is often paved with rough patches, failure, and a whole hell of a lot of hard work. That's where we shy away, turn the page, and say, "Maybe later, maybe another time."

This is when we need to fight back against those inner demons and say, "Not today! Today I start that journey. Today I lead with bravery and passion."

Historically there have always been expectations that men will accomplish great things and reach the top. They are seen as natural leaders, and accomplishment has always been highly celebrated. For women, it has been the exact opposite. Lucky for us, it's getting better and better, but the old way of thinking still exists, even if at a subconscious level.

We need to learn to celebrate our own accomplishments and victories and not diminish our power due to the opinions of others or what society has taught us to do. We also need to learn to celebrate the other women who are playing big and fully stepping into their power. Celebrate them hard! Support them, and let them know you honor their bravery and courage. No one who has ever stepped out of their comfort zone, fully walked into their ownness, taken a risk, worked their ass off, and believed in themself would ever say they regretted it. In fact, I bet they would say they would do it all over again hundredfold. To these women and other women and men in my own life, I fully honor and support you in all your accomplishments. Thank you for showing me what it means to be powerful!

I recognized that, for me, fully standing in my pow-

an infinite love

er is writing this book and taking advantage of the opportunities that arise in doing so. My power is my voice, and I plan on using it to help others live, laugh, learn, and heal. My power is being unabashedly unafraid to be me. No one else can be me better than I can. I am making a promise to myself to stay rooted in my beliefs and more grounded in nature and not to let people take advantage of my time and energy. Giving all my energy to others and not receiving what I needed in return is what got me in trouble in the first place!

Lesson one: Don't fear your own power. Fully step into its greatness.

DON'T COCOON MY BUTTERFLY

I've been told I can be intimidating. I've been told this by both men and women. Every time someone mentions that I intimidate them, I'm taken aback because I don't think I'm intimidating at all. I'm just me. Strong and confident, sure, but intimidating? At times I've also been told by people to be less *me*. Don't wear that bright lipstick color, don't brag about your accomplishments, and play down all that you take on. Don't let your personality make them feel less of.

So basically, be me, but a subdued, quiet, follow-the-rules, don't-rock-the-boat version of me. Fudge that! For too long I listened to others and put my self-worth in their hands. I forgot about myself, who I was, and what I had: a big heart, a big sense of adventure, a big dream, a big work ethic, and a big try-anything attitude.

Yes, I can be opinionated. My sister and mom say I can "get a tone" sometimes. And, yes, I can be pushy; and,

lisa beck

yes, I need to learn patience; and, yes, I need to be challenged at times. But don't cocoon my butterfly. Let me fly, baby, let me fly and watch what good I can bring into this world. If you think I'm intimidating, you should see my she-wolves! These ladies bring it with everything they've got. I learned from the best, and we support each other through it all.

Think back through your life. Has anyone in your past or present asked you to be less than you are? Whether on purpose or not, has anyone tried to cocoon your butterfly?

The first reaction to being cocooned, at least in my case, is always to feel guilty, to play the sacrificial role, and to comply with the wants and needs of others. Hello, people-pleaser personality! As I continued on my self-discovery journey, I learned to accept myself fully and to love and believe in myself fully, knowing that I had a strong, loving heart and came from a good place.

Now, when someone tells me to be less of, I generally have a few different reactions. When I have nothing invested in the relationship, I typically have a nonreaction and just say, "Byeeeee!" I recognize we are not made to be in the same orbit. For people I have ties to, I've learned to be what I call proactive rather than reactive. I step back, listen to what they are saying, and am not afraid to respectfully challenge what they say and talk about it.

More often than not, I realize they are coming from a place of self-doubt, self-fear, and self-shame. It has nothing to do with me and more to do with them. A true loved one will always want you to shine your brightest, but sometimes they can't see when their own shadowy self

an infinite love

gets in the way. I am my own hero, and no one can define my self-worth but me.

Lesson two: Fully accepting and loving yourself is not letting anyone else cast a shadow on your worth.

GIVE TO YOURSELF FIRST

I was recently listening to a podcast with Paul Chek, a fitness and holistic lifestyle guru, and he made a comment that really spoke to me. He said, "We are responsible for fifty percent of every relationship we have with someone." I started pondering this, and my internal dialogue brought up a question: *How are you showing up in this 50 percent?* Then I realized that not only are we responsible for 50 percent of every relationship we have with others, but we are 100 percent responsible for the relationship we have with ourselves. What are you bringing to the table in these relationships? Are you absolutely bringing your best self? It is up to us and us alone to figure out how we want to show up in each relationship, especially the one with ourselves.

This is our most important relationship, yet it somehow seems to be the most overlooked. Think about times you've decided you needed to fix your relationship with a friend, partner, family member, or coworker. In these situations, how many times have you turned internally and asked yourself, *What do I need to change or recognize in me first before working on my external relationships?*

For me, getting to an understanding and a *true belief* that I control and am 100-percent responsible for how I treat myself was a bit of an eye-opener. No one else should have that power over you. All too often we put all of that control in the hands of someone else. We let someone else use and abuse it. Stop! Take the power in how you treat yourself back. You own it and owe it to yourself!

It sounds like a no-brainer concept, but once drawn out on paper, how I showed up for myself looked a lot different than I'd thought. I did an experiment and created a life pie chart. I filled in percentages of who or what—work, friends, family, personal, adult responsibilities, etc.—was getting most of my energy. I then went microscopic and broke down each category even further. For example, with work, which clients took the most energy? Was this draining or fulfilling, negative or positive? And why? I asked myself, *What does my daily routine look like, and at the end of the day how do I feel? Happy, sad, uplifted, drained?*

My goal was to create a balance for myself and make sure I was putting myself and my needs first. To give myself more power. Some might say this is a selfish act, but I know deep in my heart I am not a selfish person. I'm learning to set healthy boundaries so I can live my best life and show up in each relationship, personal or professional, knowing that in the 50 percent that I am responsible for, I am giving 100 percent.

No surprise, I found that I was giving myself the least amount of energy and love. I took an inventory of which mental, physical, spiritual, and emotional needs were being met, which weren't, and what had to change in order to show up for myself 100 percent. I needed to make some changes, give less to others and more to myself, stop just dreaming, and start doing. To this day, I continue to evaluate and reevaluate as life changes. To be you is to be free.

an infinite love

Free from fear, free from self-judgment, and free to live, dream, and design the life you want to lead.

Lesson three: You are 100-percent responsible for how you show up for yourself.

OWN YOUR SEXUALITY

I believe our sexuality is connected to a fear of our power. On one hand, we are taught as young girls to tone down our sexuality, our vibrancy. On the other hand, most marketing is aimed around using our sexuality.

We are told that sexuality will bring us great things: achievements, hot men, nice cars, and vacations. Be feminine, but not too feminine. Hide your sexuality. Overexpose your sexuality to accomplish great things. Back and forth, back and forth. All of this can cause us to fear our own energy, our own vivaciousness and vitality.

As part of the confirmation curriculum in my high school religion classes, our teachers showed us a video. It was around prom time, and the video was aimed at the girls being mindful of the dresses they chose and the way they acted, as it could put the wrong type of thoughts in the minds of the boys. As if the thoughts of horny teenage boys were our fault or we had any control over them. I won't even get into all the wrong I think this video suggests, and I hope they don't make the students watch it anymore. On the upside, I also remember no one in our class, male or female, agreeing with the message the video was portraying.

I found that, once I owned my sexuality—and you can easily replace the word sexuality with "sensuality"—I became more confident in all areas of my life. I'm not talking about wearing short skirts, batting my eyelashes, and being promiscuous. I'm talking about owning and honoring my femininity. I asked myself what I enjoyed about being female and what feelings it brings out in me. What makes you feel sensual and sexual? Dancing? Cooking? A certain type of clothing? Baths? Wine and chocolates? Do more of that! Nothing makes me love and appreciate myself as a feminine more than a warm bath with a glass of wine and some candles. After the bath, I always love slathering on some sweet-smelling lotion and wrapping my body in my big, comfy robe. Do I look sexy? Probably not. Do I feel sexy? I feel absolutely female, and that to me is sexy!

Lesson four: Owning and honoring your own sexuality will increase self-confidence, add a sense of self-freedom, and boost love of self.

THE STORIES WE TELL OURSELVES

Often, our self-worth gets wrapped up in so many different situations that don't define our value as humans. We let our self-worth become defined purely by what other people say, do, think, or feel. Sometimes, even worse, we let our sense of self become determined by *the stories we tell ourselves* about what other people are thinking, doing, saying, and feeling. Here's a simple example of this that just happened to me, and I'm sure many can relate: someone said they would call me back but never did. It seems insignificant, but the stories and fabrications my ingenious mind was capable of creating as to why they didn't do as they said are novel worthy.

Reality: They forgot, they got tied up at work, they

an infinite love

got distracted. Nothing that has anything to do with me personally.

My mind: *They don't like me. I'm not worthy. They don't respect me. I did something wrong. I'm insignificant.*

I could go on and on and on. This is just one simple example, but imagine how often something like this happens. Combine it with something bigger — let's say a much more significant emotional event or trauma — and you can see how our self-worth can take a deep plummet on a regular basis all of our own doing.

The stories we tell ourselves can often be broken down into fear, shame, and unworthiness. A whole lot of "I'm not enough." Well, I'll tell you what, that's bullshit! You are enough! You always were and always will be. You are magic, and you have the magic inside you to accomplish all your hopes and dreams.

You're telling yourself one story, and you never know what story others are telling themselves. Sometimes you may not only not be on the same page but also may not even be in the same library!

I have learned to recognize this, take a step back, and ask the questions, *What story am I telling myself? Is this actually true?* Most of the time I end up giggling at the realization of how untrue the story I'm fabricating is.

This tactic has made my life 100-percent less stressful, and 100-percent happier. Insignificant situations like the one above don't bother me anymore. I am human, and self-destructive stories creep back in from time to time, but I'm now quick to recognize and resolve. Because of this, I have better relationships and conflict resolution is a hundred times easier. When dealing with conflict, I lead with the thought, *The story I'm telling myself is . . .* Or I ask them, "What is the story you are telling yourself?" I own my feelings and I talk about them.

Lesson five: You are enough. Don't let the stories you tell yourself devalue your self-worth.

EMOTIONAL SCARS WORTH HEALING

I feel so lucky to have had a really great childhood with two loving parents who honored, loved, and supported each other. They also both loved and supported my sister and me in whatever we wanted to do, but even being surrounded by all that love, no one comes out of their childhood without some emotional scars. We have to work through these scars.

Growing up, both my parents were small-business owners in our small town. Both of them worked really, really hard and emphasized the importance of hard work, being nice to others, and giving back—some really important values that I carry with me to this day.

My parents also made sure my sister and I knew that how we acted could have an immediate impact on our family and their businesses. It was important that we were smart about our decisions because it could reflect negatively on them as business owners if we weren't. Although it was not my parents' intention, these statements set up some negative associations in my development. My adult self knows they were trying to teach us about choice and that actions come with consequences. My kid self didn't see it this way.

In the back of my mind was always, *Don't mess up because it could ruin mom and dad's reputation and business and our*

an infinite love

family. You will be a big disappointment to them. You must always succeed, you must always behave, you must always follow the rules. Nice is the only way. No room for error. That's a lot of pressure to put on yourself as a young child, and to hear it reiterated (even if at a subconscious level by your own doing, as in the previous section on the stories we tell ourselves) by your role models, the people you love the most, is tough. That can leave a lot of emotional scars to work through.

At times, I still find myself fighting that battle of searching for my parents' approval and making choices that will look good in their eyes but maybe aren't exactly what I want or what is best for me.

Whose approval are you searching for? Mom, dad, sibling, partner, friends, boss? We have all searched for the approval of someone. The big question to ask yourself is why. Why are you putting so much emphasis on someone else's thoughts, words, and actions?

Battling the urge to never disappoint and to be seen as worthy and loved is another challenge for me, and probably for a lot of others. Slowly, by doing the internal work, I'm winning that battle. When I take some time to get quiet with myself and listen to my heart and soul, I find a hidden pocket of bravery and move forward. Sometimes I make a mistake, and sometimes I make the wrong choice, but I know that if I made that choice purely based on me, myself, and I, I can stand in that choice. I'm surrounded by my own love and worthiness. Your self-worth should never be wrapped up in someone else, no matter how close they are to you.

Lesson six: Never let extrinsic factors define your self-worth.

lisa beck

THE NICE GIRL

Back in college, a mentor of mine asked me to write him a brief paper on why I was so nice. I thought, *What a silly question. I'm just nice because I am!* I don't remember all that I wrote, but it was something to the tune of "I don't know how to be anything but nice. My parents emphasized the importance of niceness. I represent them and my family in my decisions."

I was labeled nice, so this is what I had to be. In my eyes, nice meant always taking care of people. Going above and beyond and not complaining. Being a yes person and a people pleaser and always willing to help out. Heaven forbid someone thought I wasn't that nice or, even worse, that I was mean. My ego would be bruised, my world shattered!

Well, no one can be "nice" all the time, and clearly I was letting other people's opinions of me really get under my skin. I also couldn't be and didn't know how to be anyone but the nice girl. Subconsciously, the only way I felt I was loved and accepted was to be nice. I recognize the juxtaposition in this: I was tired of being labeled the nice girl all the time but upset when I wasn't. Talk about a mental maze!

You're probably thinking, *Well, there are worse things to be labeled as than "nice."* You are right. Nice is wonderful, except when you have no concept of your own boundaries and your niceness gets taken advantage of. *I'll ask Lisa*, people must have thought. *She'll do it! She never says no.* And they were right; I'd never say no to anything. I was twisting myself to fit an image, and this was detrimental to my whole self and internal happiness.

an infinite love

One of my main values is freedom. Being chained to a perception of who you think you have to be isn't freeing. I had to go back and look at what emotions I was associating with this niceness label before I could move forward wholeheartedly.

When I embraced who I was and set up some healthy boundaries, I found that it truly was amazing to be a nice person, and it brought me much joy. I'm still nice—but I've learned that I can choose how, when, where, and why. That's true freedom!

Lesson seven: Being your own hero is recognizing the labels you've placed upon yourself can be altered.

RED LIPSTICK FOR THE WIN

Every time I put on red lipstick, I feel divinely feminine, badass, confident, powerful, and ready to rule the world. It's my Superman cape. I have four or five different shades because, you know, red isn't just red. Some are glossy, some matte, some long-lasting, and some I'm constantly reapplying. No matter who I'm with, I get a compliment and more often than not hear, "You can pull that off, but I never could!" My response is, "Why not? What's stopping you from rocking the red?"

Most people don't have a good response. Something to the tune of, "Oh, it's just not me!" "I don't have the face structure for it." "It's so bold. I'm not that brave." What I hear is, "I don't love myself enough to feel bold, powerful, and confident. I'm afraid of what others will think. I'll draw too much attention."

"Well," I say, "why the fudge not?" Too many of us hide our femininity and our badassness away, and it's time for the female goddess to reappear. I challenge you to give it a try and see how you feel. Do it for yourself and no one else. Put on some red lipstick, stand in front of the mirror, and really look at yourself for a good five minutes. What do you see? How do *you* feel?

Now, I don't rock the red every day, mainly because I live in workout clothes, and that would look silly. But a Friday night dinner or a power meeting? Absolutely! The color red symbolizes passion, heat, love, desire, and energy. It is highly visible and heavily used in advertisements. Red is also commonly found on many countries' flags, symbolizing courage. Hear that? Courage! Don't we all want to be courageous as we go through life?

I bring up red lipstick because, as I mentioned, it's my Superman cape. It pulls out the magical powers inside of me. If your Superman cape isn't red lipstick, what is it? A certain pair of socks, fancy blouse, or a specific song? Maybe it's a certain way you style your hair or your power briefcase. I don't care what it is. Find something that, when it's with you, near you, on you, you feel like the most confident, smartest, most badass version of yourself. Nothing can tame your wild woman ways, and by this, I mean you are confident, courageous, and on fire.

Rocking the red lipstick can also be a metaphor for life. What opportunity have you shied away from or let slip through your fingers all because you didn't believe you could do it or didn't believe you were worthy? Do not let that stop you from at least trying! Put on your Superhuman cape and rock that red. We are capable of so much more than we ever think we are. Go on and carpe diem!

an infinite love

Lesson eight: Rock the red! We all have superpowers. Find yours and use it to your advantage.

THE GRIZZLY BEAR AND THE PINE BEETLE

As I was traveling through Banff, Alberta, with my parents, we were continually on the lookout for the elusive grizzly bear. Big, strong, majestic, ferocious. One bad mama jama you wanted to see, but only at a distance. We didn't run into or even see any evidence of this massive beast, but we did see the destruction caused by another creature. The teeny-tiny, size-of-a-pencil-eraser pine beetle. These beetles had destroyed over 90 percent of the pine trees in Jasper National Park. As far as the eyes could see, the forest wasn't green but rather a brown-red, full of dead trees. A devastating blow to the ecosystem.

I bring this up because, once again, nature has taught us quite the lesson. Everyone is afraid of the big, loud grizzly, but in reality, his destruction is menial. If you don't bother him, he won't bother you. Whereas pine beetles, silent and small as they are, when joined in a common mission with other pine beetles, can take down an entire forest.

If you don't think you have a voice, if you think you don't make a difference, if you think you can't make a wave with like-minded others, you are wrong. You may be small and relatively silent in your efforts, but over time you can create massive change.

Lesson nine: Your voice matters. The small and mighty can create massive waves.

SELF-WORTH

Self-worth: It's not defined by your failures. It's not defined by your successes. It's not defined by how much money you make or how talented you are. It's not defined by being a victim or being a martyr. It's not defined by greatness or tragedy. It's not defined by the criticism, compliments, actions, or gestures of others.

Self-worth is defined by you, and it takes work! It's defined by integrity. It's defined by deep honesty and introspection. It's defined by self-respect and self-acceptance. It's defined by self-love. It's defined by courage and kindness. It's defined by vulnerability and self-happiness. Self-worth is an action verb. It's a value to always be working on.

My gratitude practice has helped to solidify my self-worth. Gratitude is attitude. Practice what you preach. If you want to have gratitude, be grateful. Gratitude is the warm sun on your face, the soft wind blowing your hair, the dog barking as you pass by, the smell of the hydrangeas blooming with butterflies floating about. Gratitude is the struggle, the fear, the pain. Embrace it all, and learn from the good, the bad, and the messy. Messy may not be fun, but it's how you learn and grow. It's how your soul evolves. Be grateful to the rain for washing away the dirt, for the fresh smell after a storm. The smell of a clean slate. In the mess is where you find your strength, your will, and your perseverance.

Lesson ten: Being your own hero is having gratitude and continually working on your own self-worth.

CALL TO ACTION

Journal about areas in your life in which you may be giving your power away.
- Ask yourself who or what is getting all your power.
- Ask yourself what boundaries you can set up to help take your power back.

List any extrinsic factors you are letting define your self-worth.

Create a gratitude practice.
- Every day, write down or say out loud at least five things you are thankful for. Bonus points if it's five characteristics or traits about yourself!

Create a life pie chart and define everything and everyone in your life that gets your time and attention.
- Who or what gets the most time?

Journal about a time when someone or something triggered insecurities or a lack of worthiness.
- What story are you telling yourself? Is there proof, or could you be way off?

Find something to be your superhero cape. Let this give you strength when you need it most.

lisa beck

Journal about any unresolved issues from your past you are carrying into your present self.
- Have you fully dealt with those old emotions and circumstances? If they keep popping up, then you haven't.

Talk with a friend or therapist about any feelings surrounding a lack of self-worth.

Read books, listen to podcasts, or watch YouTube videos on specific areas in which you need healing.

CHAPTER THIRTEEN

Be a Journey (Wo)Man

"Sometimes it's the journey that teaches you a lot about your destination."

—Drake

During graduate school, I always dreaded the end of August because it meant I had to make the 1400-mile trek from Minnesota to Massachusetts. Fortunately, I always found a road-trip partner. Most often, it was my sister, and most often we were hungover. All we could think was, *We just have to get there. Just reach our destination and all will be fine.* All I owned was in my little red Ford Escort, packed from the windows to the wall. I hated stopping, so I would make us hold our bladders until we couldn't possibly hold them anymore. The thing is, as soon as we arrived at our destination, exhausted from the drive yet elated the journey was over, we would quickly realize that one journey was over but many more—unloading the car, unpacking, and navigating a new school year—were beginning.

I think this happens to us way too often in life. We are so determined to reach our particular destination that we don't appreciate the journey to get there. We tell ourselves, *If I reach this milestone, I'll be happy. If I accomplish this goal, I'll be satisfied. If I finish this task, I'll be validated.* But are we? Sometimes, but it's often short lasting because we soon realize the end of one journey is the beginning of another. Maybe we need to stop looking at the endgame and start viewing our current scenery. What are we missing out on along the way?

When traveling through both Ireland and Denali National Park in Alaska, I remember sitting on the tour bus as we drove along an infinite number of harrowing roads on the edge of a cliff. No guardrail in sight. I would close my eyes and find myself leaning away from the window as if my hundred-and-fifty-pound body were a determining factor in whether or not our charter bus fell off the cliff. What would I have seen if, instead of being afraid and praying we reached our destination soon, I'd kept my eyes open and watched the world below me?

This chapter speaks to the journey of life we are all navigating. Some journeys are strict one-way streets. Others are a two-lane highway with a slow driver in the fast lane. And some are backcountry roads on which you go back and forth, practicing starting and stopping as you learn to drive so you can navigate the freeway unafraid. Whatever destination you choose, be sure you welcome the journey.

EXPLORE YOUR WORLD

Travel, journey, get out and about. Explore the world

an infinite love

around you. Currently, I sit on an airplane. Destination: Paris, France. One of my bucket-list destinations. I can't say why, but I was called to the city of lights, the city of love. The city of macaroons and sidewalk cafés. Notre Dame, Champs-Élysées, and Arc de Triomphe: I want to see it all. I might shed a few tears just seeing the Eiffel Tower. I am fortunate enough to have traveled a lot and have fallen in love with it. I love the excitement and preparation of planning and packing. I love immersing myself in a new culture, a new landscape, the history and stories to be told of the area.

I love starting out my journey, getting to the airport early and enjoying a glass of bubbly as I watch the people around me and ask myself, *What's their story? Where are they going? Are they traveling for business? Pleasure? What are they doing in my departing city?*

When traveling for pleasure, I think it's important to experience two different types of travel. One is with a group, large or small, of friends or family. You will quickly find out how you travel and whom you travel with best. Sometimes the people closest to you are the hardest to travel with. Go figure! This experience will teach you patience and will open your eyes to many different quirks in yourself and others. Besides, shared experiences, whether they are good or bad, always enhance connection. Let us remember connection is the one trait we as humans all crave.

The second experience I believe everyone should have at least once in their lifetime is solo travel. There's no better time to learn who you are and what you are capable of. Traveling alone will make you step out of your comfort zone, and we all know life is more exciting one step outside of the comfort zone. Explore your surroundings and explore yourself. Two of the best trips I've ever been on, I traveled alone. Navigate your surroundings and communicate with others. Sit at a café and watch the world go by.

Slow down, take in nature, and observe others. Start a conversation. I have a dear friend who emulates this in everyday life. Her stories of people, cultures, and lessons learned are epic. She's compassionate, inquisitive, and always respectful. I've never met another person more understanding of others, different cultures, and how the world works. Travel changes you.

I certainly understand traveling, whether it be in a group or solo, takes a certain level of financial means. But don't let this stop you from exploring the world around you. If air travel is not your thing, take a train, a bus, or a drive to a city, big or small, that you haven't been to. Take an hour, a day, a week, or a month and explore.

Why is it that the most we explore our own city is when someone from out of state comes to visit? It doesn't cost a thing for us to hop on a bike and ride to a different neighborhood, sit in a park, and read a book. Maybe we aren't traveling far, but that's not the point. The point is to get out of our comfort zone, to do something different, to spend some time learning about ourselves.

If you are feeling "stuck" in your life, the best way to get unstuck is to learn about yourself. Take some quality time away with yourself. When I traveled to Costa Rica and to Kenora, Ontario, and immersed myself in my environment and in the purpose of my retreats, it changed my life. The people I met from around the world became

an infinite love

family, and my personal growth was exponential. I came back a better version of myself.

Lesson one: Whether your travel plans are big or small, take time to explore the world around you. Travel is a great teacher.

GO ON A MENTAL JOURNEY

If you want to grow as a person, take a journey. We just talked about the benefits of taking a physical journey, but you can also take a mental journey. Learn a new language, take a course, attempt a new hobby, or read a book that challenges your ideals. Challenge your body to challenge your mind. Have you ever tried to learn a dance routine? When I was little, my sister and I, along with our neighborhood gang, loved to make up dance routines. It's physically demanding and mentally exhausting! Hop in a new fitness class or go for a run. Pushing yourself physically demands mental toughness.

You won't grow unless you challenge yourself because it's in the challenge that we learn and prosper. When have you challenged yourself? Was it a positive or negative experience? How did you grow? What did you learn about yourself, good or bad?

Remember that golf league I previously mentioned. Well, I was nervous to start and warned my foursome that I was a newbie to the sport. They reminded me they were all new to the sport at one time as well. The ladies have been so supportive and helped me to improve my game. We have a lot of fun and always make time to enjoy some chitchat, coffee, and cookies after our early morning round. I have so much fun with them that I decided to join another league at a different course.

As I was signing up for my Wednesday afternoon league, the Golf Pro notified me that it was a co-ed league and there were seventy men signed up and only two women. I looked at him and said, "Ah, no worries. I'm up for the challenge!" I have moments of brilliance on the course—and, in my mind, I'm a fabulous golfer—but on paper and in all actuality, I'm still way, way, way a novice. As I got home, full panic set in. *Oh dear lord, what have I just done? I, a novice golfer, just signed up for what is basically a men's league at a course I have never played before!* Nothing like jumping in feet first and blind. Then I started laughing out loud because that was so typical of me. I realized I'm pretty fearless—that, or I don't have a lot of critical-thinking skills. Run a half marathon when the most training you've done is one five-mile jog? Check. Do a 125-mile ride for charity on a bike with no road training? Check, although I do not recommend!

No matter the outcome, I'm up for the challenge, as I know only growth is possible.

Lesson two: Taking a journey that challenges you mentally or physically will lead to personal growth and development, creating a deeper appreciation of self.

FEAR, SHMEAR

As I was nearing the end of writing this book, I sent a group text to my support posse, a.k.a. my sexy six girl gang. "Only two chapters left to write on the book! Send high vibes for me to get this baby wrapped up!"

Obviously, I received a lot of "Go girl!", "You can do

an infinite love

it!", and "Woot woot!" High-fives and heart emojis too. But what I didn't expect was the "I'm so proud of you, I could never write a book!", "OMG how scary to write a book!", "Girl, you're so brave!", and so on. It never occurred to me that writing a book could be scary or that I was somehow being brave. Maybe that's because I was in the middle of it and, as immensely proud of myself as I was for setting a goal and working toward accomplishing it, I was totally ready to be done writing and get this masterpiece out into the world for other people to read. Fear never crossed my mind. For me, it was a journey. Writing this book has been an exciting, albeit nerve-racking and at times frustrating, self-realizing journey that I had to go on. For that I am eternally grateful. Maybe writing a book sounds daunting and scary to them, but performing surgery, being a CIO of a corporation, traveling to remote areas of the world, and all the other courageous and brave things these ladies do on a regular basis all seem scary to me!

The point being, everything's scary in the beginning, and that's because *we* make it so. You can make something so large and so overwhelming in your mind that fear and a little, or a lot, of anxiety are the only emotions you are capable of holding. No matter what the circumstance, don't let fear take the wheel. Just remember, the thought of starting something new or challenging is scarier than actually doing it. When you're in it, you're just in it! One day at a time. Deep breaths, meditation, and a hefty support posse can get you through anything. Many times, the harder the journey, the sweeter the success.

How often have you held back and not jumped in

because of fear? Stop making the journey bigger than it needs to be. Practice patience and focus on your self-belief. You are enough! Maybe all will work out well in the end, and maybe it will be a real damn struggle. Either way, celebrate the fact that you took the leap. Good or bad, what are the lessons you learned along the way?

Lesson three: The road may be littered with potholes and sharp turns, but don't let fear stand in the way of reaching your destination.

CALL TO ACTION

Journal about areas in your life in which you can slow down and appreciate the ride instead of only seeing the destination.

Plan a trip with friends or family.
- Whether it be an afternoon in a neighboring town or a journey halfway around the world, get out of your routine and take time to connect with others.

Plan a solo journey.

Challenge yourself mentally and physically. Make a list of all the things you've always thought about doing but never did because the scaries crept in.
- Pick one and take one step toward that goal today.

CHAPTER FOURTEEN

Cultivate Connection

"Carve your name on hearts, and not on marble."
—Charles Spurgeon

Dan Buettner, author of *Blue Zones*, a book studying the areas of the world that have the most centenarians, notes that one of the commonalities among Blue Zones is a cultural emphasis on connection—connection through family, community, faith, and finding your right social circle. Brené Brown repeatedly speaks to the importance of connection in order to live wholeheartedly. Johann Hari, an author and speaker who studies addiction, believes addiction is a problem of disconnection and not being able to be present in one's own life. He says the opposite of addiction isn't getting sober; it's creating bonds and connections. I believe it's a connection to yourself, others, and the world around you.

Currently, as a society, we are the most connected we've ever been, yet the face-to-face human connection we once had has decreased. Hari references a study by environmental writer Bill McKibben noting that the number of close friends we can call on during a crisis has dwindled

an infinite love

since 1950, yet the amount of floor space and stuff we've acquired has been increasing. As a result, we may be one of the loneliest societies to date. Deepening our connection to one another will help us all create infinite love for ourselves.

FAMILY TRADITIONS

I come from a large extended family, both on my mother's side and father's side. I feel blessed and honestly wouldn't want it any other way. Both sides of my family are entirely different, yet both value connections and are so loving in their own individual way. We've lost a few members over the years, but both sides of my family recognized early on the importance of the love and support a family can offer. Both sets of grandparents passed way too young and, to this day, each side makes a conscious effort to continue to gather and keep relationships alive.

This effort has had a huge impact on me. I see the bond my parents have with their siblings, and it's important for me to have the same with my sister. As a youngster, watching my older cousins and seeing them as role models made me want to be a role model to their children and my younger cousins. In all times, good and bad, we show up for each other to celebrate the wins and hold hands during the losses.

Every summer for as long as I've been alive, my dad's side of the family has gathered at my aunt and uncle's cabin for an annual bocce ball tournament. What started as a leisurely way to pass the time as dinner was being cooked has turned into a serious tournament with official rules, a winner's plaque, and bragging rights. I love this fun, competitive tradition we've started, and everyone looks forward to this weekend throughout the year. We all lead busy lives and there never seem to be enough summer weekends, but every family member makes this weekend a priority. We find value in the tradition, love the continual reconnection, and understand the importance of investing time into family.

My mother's side of the family lives all over the country and even the world yet has gathered to spend four to five days together every other year for the past thirty. We laugh, we cook, we play, and we have epic bonfires. I love the relationships I have formed with each individual aunt, uncle, and cousin. We have such varied backgrounds, journeys, and locations, but the determination, individuality, work ethic, love, and support I have learned from these people are bar none. Cream of the crop.

I'm so grateful my family keeps traditions alive and makes the choice to spend time with each other. Although I happen to come from a large extended genetic family, I truly believe family is family no matter if they are related to you or not. If you don't have a large biological family or maybe just not a great relationship with them, don't let that stop you. Create your family with whomever you wish: friends, neighbors, other loved ones, and even pets. Family is family and love is love. The important part is making a continued effort to connect with loved ones. What traditions can you start that will carry on from generation to generation?

Lesson one: Make family a priority. Gather your family and start a tradition.

an infinite love

HERE A FRIEND, THERE A FRIEND, EVERYWHERE A FRIEND

I recently attended a book signing event to listen to the author speak. I took a seat, not paying much mind to where or who I was sitting next to. Before I knew it, the two women next to me and I started chatting. They were two young women recently out of college and heading into full-on adult life. Both traveled to the book event by themselves, and they openly admitted they were nervous and weren't even sure if they should attend because they had to come alone. Call it independence, life lessons learned, age, or maturity, but it didn't even occur to me that I was also by myself. I wanted to go to the book event, so I went and didn't even bat an eye that I wasn't with anyone.

When they found out that I was a wise old woman in my midthirties, they started asking me all these questions. The main thing they wanted to know was how to make friends now that they were out of college and into the working world. I had to chuckle because, in their eyes, I could see exactly where I was at twenty-three. Full of hope and wonder but also afraid and realizing life post-college could be difficult.

College itself is a social network. There are always people around to do something with, people to go out to eat with, groups to join, and social events to attend. If you live in a dorm, frat, or sorority or are on a sports team, there are given friends at every moment of the day. As college ends, your social circle dramatically decreases as people follow different paths. Some continue with school, others with internships. Some travel, and others enter the workforce. Meeting new friends post-school is like dating.

You have to put yourself out there. Join a club or organization, make an effort to meet and mingle with coworkers, and step outside of your box. Every young person is in the same situation as you. Be open-minded and accepting of everyone. You will click better with some than others, and pretty soon you will find your tribe and have a brand-new social circle.

Lesson two: Sometimes connecting with others means taking a giant step outside your comfort zone.

FIND YOUR TRIBE

"Find your tribe" is a pretty common saying as of late, but the concept has been around forever. In ancient times, women would gather to support each other as the men went off to war or the hunt. We as humans have always had a need to connect, but in today's society I think we make it difficult for ourselves. In ancient times, connection was also about survival. There were no walls built up, everyone had a role to play, and support was the name of the game.

Today we are busy running here, there, and everywhere. We are lucky that technology has made survival much easier, but it has also lessened our connections with others. Because we still crave connection, even if it's just subconsciously, we automatically turn to our partners. However, our partners can't be our tribe. They may be able to fulfill a few aspects, but one person can't be everything to another. Those are some big shoes to fill, and this expectation can put stress on the relationship. When we have a collective group we can turn to, we lessen the stress on our relationships.

an infinite love

I have many different groups in my own life, including those I discuss spiritual matters with, those that I connect with over health and wellness, the group that enjoys the same passions as me, and the friends that have been with me since childhood. All these groups are equally important and fulfill major roles in my life, and asking one person to handle all these roles seems absurd! Yet we do it all the time.

Lesson three: A tribe consists of many. Don't expect one person to be it all.

DEFINING YOUR SOCIAL CIRCLES

It's important you define the social circles you have in your life and the different roles they play. Make sure you are clear on your expectations of each group and set boundaries if needed. You don't want to expect more from someone than they are willing to give. I wouldn't go to my golf friends, most of whom are men, and talk to them about the struggles I'm having with menstrual cramps. I will, however, chat with them about the latest sports scores. We discussed in a previous chapter the importance of defining the roles you play in life, and it's equally important to define your different social circles and the roles they play.

Lesson four: Being crystal clear on expectations from each social group will set you up for better connections and lessen disappointments.

THAT ONE GROUP

As I sat there at the book event chatting with these two lovely strangers about making friends, I started thinking about my own social circles and connections. I have a group of girlfriends—my sexy six, as I call them—that I've been friends with since childhood. Five out of the six of us grew up within a two-block radius of each other.

I think back on our history, and frankly I'm amazed that we are all still such a tight friend group. We never all participated in the same sports or activity, our parents weren't all in the same friend group, we didn't go to the same colleges, our interests are very different, and at no point since graduating high school have all six of us even lived in the same city. Yet we value our connection and are closer now than we have ever been. This is also because we make a concerted effort to remain connected. Jobs have relocated my sexy six to random cities across the states, but for one long weekend each year, we gather to eat, drink, act like teenagers, and reconnect. This reconnection is vital for each of us in many different ways, as each of us brings our own unique gifts to our friendship.

This was never more evident to me than during our 2018 girls' getaway. Over the past couple of years, I've uncovered some unique gifts. My intuition is spot on, and I can feel people's energies and the energy of the world around me. Other times I know random things, such as who's going to win a game, who's sending me a text or call before my phone even beeps, and the gender of a baby in utero. I can't explain how I know, but with all of me, I just know. The biggest gift I've come to realize is the fact that I can feel when someone connected to me passes away. I can feel their soul transition. A friend's father, my aunt, a client's mother. I've come to understand my gift of feeling is to help others heal. As I learned to navigate these gifts, I was nervous to talk about it with my girl tribe. Why? I

an infinite love

was worried they would think I was making this stuff up or that I was a crazy lady. Subconsciously, I think I was worried I no longer belonged and would be abandoned. I became real emotional and started crying as I explained my newly discovered gifts—gifts that I believed I'd always had but was just awakening to. I started crying because I realized they weren't kicking me out or abandoning me. They were curious, wanted to try to understand, and loved me all the same.

It was in this moment that I came to understand that, for a tribe to really cultivate deep connection, each person must be 100-percent authentic. All masks must come off. Your go-to group must lift each other up and support one another through love and respect. Always create a safe space for sharing that holds everyone accountable and pushes them to learn and grow. Take a look at your own close group of friends. Do they honor these values? If they don't, then you may need to find a different tribe or redefine the role this tribe plays in your life.

Lesson five: Sometimes finding and connecting with that one group takes a lot of effort, and in order to harbor deep connections with your tribe, each person must be fully authentic. Your uniqueness only adds to the group.

VOLUNTEER

I can never emphasize enough the importance of volunteering. Anytime I volunteer, I always leave feeling better than when I arrived. Volunteering can help you connect with complete strangers, your local community, and yourself. I spent many years volunteering on a regular basis, and all my connections were joyous ones. As I started writing this section, I felt like a bit of a fraud because I was talking about the importance of volunteering and, there I sat, not actively volunteering for an organization anymore. It then hit me that volunteering doesn't have to be so large or with a major organization. I actually volunteer all the time. I volunteer to watch my nephew and niece. I volunteer to stay a bit after a workout session with a client and help move furniture or carry heavy boxes. I volunteer to run an errand for a client. I volunteer to work with a friend and break down his golf swing. And so on.

Make a conscious effort to start volunteering. It doesn't have to be a large contribution. Any effort counts and establishes a connection you may have missed out on.

Lesson six: Create connection in your community by volunteering.

CALL TO ACTION

Make a list of your current family traditions.
- How can you honor these more?
- If you don't have any traditions, create one.

Write down your current social groups and the names of the people you hang out with the most. Answer the following questions.
- What roles do each of these groups play in your life? Are expectations defined and boundaries clear?
- Do you have a close group (more than one person) that lovingly supports you and offers you guidance?
- Do they have your back through thick and thin?
- Are you able to be vulnerable and share from the heart with each other?

List ways you can connect more with the people in your tribe.

Make a point to connect with a group of friends.

Plan a weekend getaway with your girl group.

List ways you can volunteer more in your community or for others.

Conclusion

During my time in Kenora, Mark—our dynamic leadership coach and an author and speaker who teaches high-performance leadership development to different companies around the globe—loved to challenge us by putting our head in a mental pretzel. One afternoon he gave us a scenario: We were head of the FBI, boarding a plane to drop off money and negotiate with a terrorist group to get the president's daughter back. In our hypothetical situation, we didn't know if we would make it back alive and had fifteen minutes to write a letter to someone, anyone. Who would you write to? What would you say to them? These were the questions we had to quickly think about. How can you possibly say enough in fifteen minutes?

I sat down to write, and my pen started flowing. I wasn't even thinking, just writing, and everything came tumbling out. When time was up, I reread what I wrote and realized I didn't write my letter to anyone in particular. It was universal. It was to anyone and everyone. If my plane were to go down tomorrow, this is my wish for you:

"You are loved unconditionally through and through. There is nothing in this entire world that you cannot accomplish. Believe in yourself and believe in your full potential. Find your passion and do just that. Live it, feel

an infinite love

it, breathe it in. Let it consume you, let it enrapture you. Carry that with you wherever you go.

"Find love, love yourself beyond all else, and find the courage to love others with a full heart and an open mind. Be yourself in any situation. Live authentically and look for authenticity in others. Forgive! Forgive your past, forgive your present. Set intentions to forgive in the future. Forgive yourself, forgive others. Let the pain, the hurt, the guilt, let it go. Let it go. You are human just like everyone else. Be kind, show kindness.

"Travel, see the world, don't just look at the surface, dig deep. Explore the unexplored. Be a journeyman. Find the journey. Go on the journey. Take off the mask, be vulnerable. Open your heart and your mind. That's where growth is, that's being brave, that's walking in the face of danger. That's the juicy part, the sweet nectar of life.

"Live your life right. Be a good friend, sister, brother, father, son, mother, daughter. Show support, listen more, and talk less. See, really see the world around you. See others. Take care of the environment. Respect yourself enough to respect the earth.

"Take care of your health. Move your body, challenge your mind, eat right. Find emotional intelligence. Go to the doctor, take the needed rest. Relax. Find what lights you up. Do that . . . more of that. Be happy. Forget the bullshit. Be happy. Spread happiness to others.

"Try everything, food, sports, music, art, education. Give it all a chance. Clean your room. Keep a clean place. Protect yourself, protect yourself financially, energetically, environmentally. Wear sunscreen. Get out in nature. Walk in the woods. Hear the birds, feel the sun, smell the

lisa beck

woods, listen to the wind blow the trees. Take time to rest. Sleep seven to nine hours a night. Take a nap. Let your body repair.

"Be selfish with your time but don't forget to give. Be independent, not dependent. Nourish your body and soul. Read, write, find a creative outlet. Be proud of yourself, where you've come from, where you are now and where you are going. Slow down. Be in the present. Learn from the past but don't dwell on it. Look forward to the future but don't let it consume you. Be in the present. You are a unique, gifted, loved individual with so much power to really make an impact so go out there and LIVE!"

As I journeyed through the process of writing my book, I realized I had a choice. I had a choice to lead the most dynamic, awesome, joyous life filled with connection, authenticity, passion, and love. This choice may come easy to some and harder to others, as it involves going deep within yourself, doing the work, getting vulnerable, and asking the hard questions: *What am I afraid of? Where does this stem from? Am I being completely honest with myself? What events from my childhood are affecting my actions and decisions in adulthood? What do I value? Am I judging myself too harshly and therefore afraid of others' judgment? Etc.* At the end of the day, it all comes down to love. The sooner we let go of our fear, forgive ourselves, and fully realize and step into our power, the sooner we can create an intimate love within our hearts.

I will leave you with this: In order to give, give to yourself first. In order to forgive, forgive yourself first. In order to love, love yourself first! May you surround yourself with infinite love inside and out.

Acknowledgments

All the things, events, people in your life are supposed to be there. There are no random encounters, only synchronicities. People who have made a lasting impression in your life, good or bad, were there to help or teach you a lesson you chose to learn well beyond this lifetime. It took me a hot minute to recognize this in my own life. As I was wrapping up the first draft of this book I came to realize all the events, people, places, and lessons learned that led to me writing it. Without these lessons, without these people, this book would not be possible. To my parents, who—unbeknownst to them—are brought up a lot throughout this book and taught me what the love of a family truly looks like. My sister and bestest friend in the world, who's my sounding board for everything. My best friend, Carrie, who is spontaneous enough to get a random tattoo with me, as I know it wouldn't have been something I'd have done alone at the time. She also pulled me aside when I graduated from college and said, "You are starting to invest your money now. Whatever you can afford to invest each month, do it!" Without my financial adviser, Ryan, helping me to make smart financial decisions, I wouldn't have been able to fund the publication of this book. His gifts are helping me to fund mine. Without the journey I've been on, I'd never have met the incredible people in my life that taught me lessons I've needed to learn, opened my eyes to a different mindset or new way of seeing things, challenged me when I needed to be challenged, and supported me when I needed the support. Many whom I've mentioned throughout the book and many whom I haven't, but whose spirits were with me within each chapter. To all of you, for all of this, I'm eternally grateful.

About the Author

LISA BECK has been involved in the health and fitness industry since 2000. With a bachelor of science degree in athletic training, she has spent many sports seasons helping athletes prevent, manage, and rehabilitate injuries. She continued her education receiving her master's degree in sports and event management. Lisa is a certified personal trainer, corrective exercise specialist, functional nutrition specialist, golf swing specialist, reflexive performance reset certified, rocktape certified, and TRX certified. She has a passion for understanding and learning how the body moves and how to help people feel better. When she's not working with clients, Lisa delves into leadership coaching, helping to cultivate culture, communication, and leadership in men, women, and youth. When she's taking time to fulfill her soul, you will find Lisa writing, traveling, golfing, working on self-development, playing with her niece and nephew, and loving on her dog, Daks. She calls Minneapolis home.